I0037744

R

PROGRAMMING

R BASICS FOR BEGINNERS

Andy Vickler

© Copyright 2022 - All rights reserved.

The contents of this book may not be reproduced, duplicated, or transmitted without direct written permission from the author.

Under no circumstances will any legal responsibility or blame be held against the publisher for any reparation, damages, or monetary loss due to the information herein, either directly or indirectly.

Legal Notice:

You cannot amend, distribute, sell, use, quote, or paraphrase any part of the content within this book without the consent of the author.

Disclaimer Notice:

Please note the information contained within this document is for educational and entertainment purposes only. No warranties of any kind are expressed or implied. Readers acknowledge that the author is not engaging in the rendering of legal, financial, medical, or professional advice. Please consult a licensed professional before attempting any techniques outlined in this book.

By reading this document, the reader agrees that under no circumstances is the author responsible for any losses, direct or indirect, which are incurred as a result of the use of the information contained within this document, including, but not limited to, —errors, omissions, or inaccuracies.

Table of Contents

Introduction

This paper aims to offer a starting point for persons who are new to R. I opted to focus on learning how R works since I wanted to teach it to beginners rather than experts. Given the breadth of R's capabilities, it's beneficial for a beginner to grasp some fundamental ideas and notions to progress quickly. We attempted to make the descriptions as simple as possible so that they would be understandable to everyone while also providing useful details, sometimes in the form of tables and pictures.

In the following chapters, we will discuss the basic building blocks of the R Programming language. R programming is also called the data science language, created by statisticians as a Go-To language. Following is the chart created by a data science expert, showing the usage of the R program is the first one rating more than python.

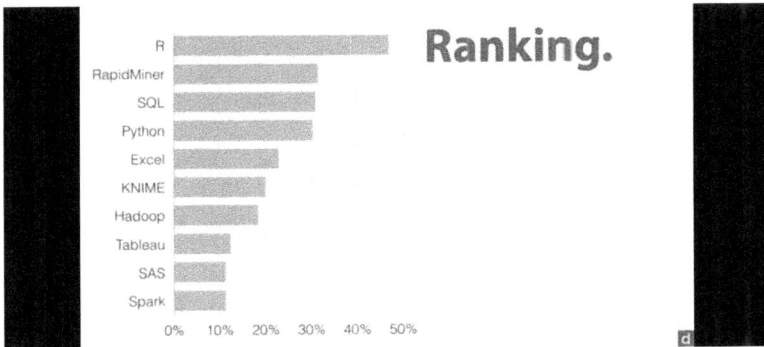

"Ross Ihaka" and "Robert Gentleman" invented "R," a statistical analysis and graphics system. R is a programming language and a "dialect" of the S programming developed by "AT&T Bell Laboratories." "S" is accessible as part of the Insightful S-PLUS software package. The designs of R and S differ significantly; anyone interested in learning more might read the article by Ihaka & Gentleman, a copy of which is also supplied with R.

The GNU General Public License allows R to be freely distributed. The R Development Core Team is a group of statisticians who work on its development and dissemination.

R is accessible in various formats, including the source code (written primarily in C with some Fortran functions), which is mainly for "Unix" and "Linux machines," and "pre-compiled binaries for Windows, Linux, and Macintosh."

So why is R becoming a useful tool in data and statistics analysis?

There are many reasons for that, and it's impossible to mention all of them. Following are some of the main reasons for the R program's popularity among other programs.

1. It is free and open-source.

2. It is optimized for vector operations. We will discuss this later in the book.

3. A huge community of tech and support is there to help you.

4. It has over 9000 contributive packages, which gives you so many options—all free.

This book will teach the value of R Programming and its benefits for solving complex data problems. On top of this, you will understand the core elements of R while also learning the process of analyzing your data via the data analysis process. You will go through importing your data into R. You will then learn to clean and transform the data to a more usable format. You will learn to understand and create powerful graphics and visuals that express your data and its story in compelling ways while creating reproducible code to share with others.

R may appear to be too complicated for a non-specialist at first. This may not be the case. R's versatility is, in fact, one of its most conspicuous features. Whereas traditional software instantly presents a study's findings, R keeps these outcomes in an "object," allowing a study to be completed without any results being presented. This may startle the user. However, the aforesaid function is really valuable.

Certainly, the operator can <u>abstract</u> merely the relevant portion of the "results."

For example, suppose one performs a sequence of 30 regressions and wishes to compare the different regression coefficients. In that case, R can display simply the predicted figures, but traditional software would open 30 results windows. Other examples will demonstrate the versatility of a system like "R" compared to traditional software.

R performs all of its operations on objects in the computer's active memory; no momentary files are needed. File readings and writing are utilized for data and result from input and output (graphics, . . .). The user carries out the functions via a set of instructions. The outcomes are shown on the computer screen, saved as an "object" or "written on a disc" (especially in the case of graphics). Because the findings are things in and of themselves, they may be treated as data and analyzed. Data files can be read from a local disc or via the internet from a distant server.

Chapter 1

Getting started

What is R?

So you have decided that you would like to begin programming. Choosing a programming language to start with can be an extremely daunting decision. Rest assured, the R programming language is an excellent place to begin.

In 1993, Ross lhaka and Robert Gentleman developed the language and named it R language. This tool was considered one of the best tools for data processing due to its huge storage It can easily handle a huge amount of data. That is why every fortune company, such as Facebook, Uber, Airbnb, etc., uses it to build their application. The founders made it easy to understand. They had in mind that every kind of industry would use it.

Created as an open-source implementation of the S programming language, R has deep roots in statistics and academia. Because of the intended user base of R, the language is designed to make it extremely easy for people with little-to-no computer programming knowledge to pick up the language and begin programming quickly. The ease of use and availability of the language, combined with its base and emphasis on data analysis and statistics, is why R continues to be the dominant programming language for statisticians, analysts, and data miners worldwide.

How Does R work

The point that "R" is a "programming language" may put off many people who believe they cannot "program." For two reasons, this should not be the case. To begin, R is an inferred rather than a compiled language, which means that any instructions written on the keyboard are immediately performed without the need to create a whole program, as is the case with other computer languages.

Second, R's syntax is straightforward and easy to understand. For example, the function "lm(y x")" means "fitting a linear model with y as response and x as a predictor," which means "fitting a linear model with y as response and x as a predictor." A function must always be written with parentheses to be performed in R. Even if there is nothing within them, "R" will show the contented task if the function's name is typed without parentheses. Unless the text clearly indicates otherwise, the names of the functions are placed in parenthesis in this document to distinguish them from other objects.

Variables, functions, data, results, and other items are saved in the computer's dynamic memory as objects with names when R is operating.

The user may perform operations on these observations with different "operators" "(arithmetic, logical, comparison, etc.)" and many other functions. The usage of operators is rather simple; we'll go over the details later.

Preparing Our System for "R"

Before installing the program, you must meet the system requirements. You must make sure that your system meets the minimum hardware requirements of the program defined below.

- The R program is built for both 32bit and 64bit platforms. Along with x86-compatible architecture

- For windows users: windows 10, windows server 2012, and 2016 are required

- Linus: "Ubuntu 16.04,18.04 , CentOS/Red Hat Enterprise Linux 7 .x, 8.x" and SUSE Linus Enterprise server 12, 15

- Multiple core chips are recommended.

- 256 MB of free disk space (RAM)

- RAM should be 4GB at least.

Installing R

To begin using R, you must first install it on your computer system. Thankfully, installing the language is incredibly simple and quick whether you are an avid Windows, macOS, or Linux user. Due to the similarities in the process between Windows and macOS, this book has combined the two into a single guide. Linux-based users are instructed to navigate to the CRAN Linux installation page (https://cran.r-project.org/bin/linux/) to find detailed instructions on installing R based on common Linux distributions.

Installing R on Windows or macOS

While there are a few different methods of installing the R language to your Windows or macOS system, this guide will focus on using the Comprehensive R Archive Network (commonly shortened as CRAN). CRAN is an incredible resource in the R community and acts as an ever-evolving archive for R and its core packages.

1. In your preferred web browser, navigate to the CRAN webpage (https://cran.r-project.org/), where you should see this page below.

2. You will select the appropriate link from this screen based on whether you are using a Windows or macOS computer. Depending on which system download link you have chosen, you will be taken to one of these two pages seen on the next page.

Windows Users:

R for Windows

Subdirectories:

base   Binaries for base distribution. This is what you want to install R for the first time.
contrib   Binaries of contributed CRAN packages (for R >= 2.13.x; managed by Uwe Ligges). There is also information on third party software available for CRAN Windows
              services and corresponding environment and make variables.
old contrib   Binaries of contributed CRAN packages for outdated versions of R (for R < 2.13.x; managed by Uwe Ligges).
Rtools   Tools to build R and R packages. This is what you want to build your own packages on Windows, or to build R itself.

Please do not submit binaries to CRAN. Package developers might want to contact Uwe Ligges directly in case of questions / suggestions related to Windows binaries.

You may also want to read the R FAQ and R for Windows FAQ.

Note: CRAN does some checks on these binaries for viruses, but cannot give guarantees. Use the normal precautions with downloaded executables.

macOS Users:

R for macOS

This directory contains binaries for a base distribution and packages to run on macOS. Releases for old Mac OS X systems (through Mac OS X 10.5) and PowerPC Macs can be found in the old directory.

Note: Although we take precautions when assembling binaries, please use the normal precautions with downloaded executables.

Package binaries for R versions older than 3.2.0 are only available from the CRAN archive so users of such versions should adjust the CRAN mirror setting (https://cran-archive.r-project.org) accordingly.

R 4.1.2 "Bird Hippie" released on 2021/11/01

Please check the SHA1 checksum of the downloaded image to ensure that it has not been tampered with or corrupted during the mirroring process. For example type
openssl sha1 R-4.1.2.pkg
in the Terminal application to print the SHA1 checksum for the R-4.1.2.pkg image. On Mac OS X 10.7 and later you can also validate the signature using
pkgutil --check-signature R-4.1.2.pkg

Latest release:

R-4.1.2.pkg (notarized and signed)   R 4.1.2 binary for macOS 10.13 (High Sierra) and higher, Intel 64-bit build, signed and notarized package.
SHA1-hash: 01d6909aa70f5b44e5a2e467200fba040f9baa   Contains R 4.1.2 framework, R.app GUI 1.77 in 64-bit for Intel Macs, Tcl/Tk 8.6/6 X11 libraries and Texinfo 6.7. The latter two components are
(ca. 87MB)   optional and can be ommitted when choosing "custom install", they are only needed if you want to use the tcltk R package or build package
                                         documentation from sources.

                                         Note: the use of X11 (including tcltk) requires XQuartz to be installed since it is no longer part of OS X. Always re-install XQuartz when
                                         upgrading your macOS to a new major version.

                                         This release supports Intel Macs, but it is also known to work using Rosetta2 on M1-based Macs. For native Apple silicon arm64 binary see
                                         below.

                                         Important: this release uses Xcode 12.4 and GNU Fortran 8.2. If you wish to compile R packages from sources, you may need to download GNU
                                         Fortran 8.2 - see the tools directory.

R-4.1.2-arm64.pkg (notarized and signed) R 4.1.2 binary for macOS 11 (Big Sur) and higher, Apple silicon arm64 build, signed and notarized package.
SHA1-hash: 4bef84f9b134c312a84edc34512e041ebeea3   Contains R 4.1.2 framework, R.app GUI 1.77 for Apple silicon Macs (M1 and higher), Tcl/Tk 8.6.11 X11 libraries and Texinfo 6.7.
(ca. 87MB)   Important: this version does NOT work on older Intel-based Macs.

                                         Note: the use of X11 (including tcltk) requires XQuartz. Always re-install XQuartz when upgrading your macOS to a new major version.

                                         This release uses Xcode 12.4 and experimental GNU Fortran 11 arm64 fork. If you wish to compile R packages from sources, you may need to
                                         download GNU Fortran for arm64 from https://mac.R-project.org/libs-arm64. Any external libraries and tools are expected to live in /opt/R
                                         /arm64 to not conflict with Intel-based software and this build will not use /usr/local to avoid such conflicts.

3. If you are installing the program for the first, you will need to download b in both operating systems.

   a. For Windows users, you will navigate to the "base" subdirectory, where you can download the current base R .exe installer. Download the current version of R as shown highlighted in the image below.

Download R 4.1.2 for Windows (86 megabytes, 32/64 bit)

Installation and other instructions
New features in this version

If you want to double-check that the package you have downloaded matches the package distributed by CRAN, you can compare the md5sum of the .exe to the fingerprint on the master server. You will need a version of md5sum for windows: both graphical and command line versions are available.

Frequently asked questions

- Does R run under my version of Windows?
- How do I update packages in my previous version of R?
- Should I run 32-bit or 64-bit R?

Please see the R FAQ for general information about R and the R Windows FAQ for Windows-specific information.

Other builds

- Patches to this release are incorporated in the r-patched snapshot build.
- A build of the development version (which will eventually become the next major release of R) is available in the r-devel snapshot build.
- Previous releases

Note to webmasters: A stable link which will redirect to the current Windows binary release is
<CRAN MIRROR>/bin/windows/base/release.html.

b. macOS users have a slightly different approach to downloading their version of base R as two different options vary on which CPUtheir Apple mac computer has been installed. An easy way to verify which download link is right for you is by checking which CPU your macOS computer has installed in it. You can do this quickly by going to the "About This Mac" menu found by clicking the Apple found in the Menu Bar.

c. Intel-based Mac computer users will need to download the link highlighted in yellow, while arm-based mac users will need to download the link highlighted in green.

R for macOS

This directory contains binaries for a base distribution and packages to run on macOS. Releases for old Mac OS X systems (through Mac OS X 10.5 and PowerPC Macs can be found in the old directory.

Note: Although we take precautions when assembling binaries, please use the normal precautions with downloaded executables.

Package binaries for R versions older than 3.2.0 are only available from the CRAN archive so users of such versions should adjust the CRAN mirror setting (https://cran-archive.r-project.org) accordingly.

R 4.1.2 "Bird Hippie" released on 2021/11/01

Please check the SHA1 checksum of the downloaded image to ensure that it has not been tampered with or corrupted during the mirroring process. For example type
openssl shal R-4.1.2.pkg
in the *Terminal* application to print the SHA1 checksum for the R-4.1.2.pkg image. On Mac OS X 10.7 and later you can also validate the signature using
pkgutil --check-signature R-4.1.2.pkg

Latest release:

R-4.1.2.pkg (notarized and signed)
SHA1-hash: 81e2b69eec78f5b8c5a2b9b72990a4686aaa
(ca. 87MB)

R 4.1.2 binary for macOS 10.13 (**High Sierra**) and higher, **Intel 64-bit** build, signed and notarized package. Contains R 4.1.2 framework, R.app GUI 1.77 in 64-bit for Intel Macs, Tcl/Tk 8.6.6 X11 libraries and Texinfo 6.7. The latter two components are optional and can be omitted when choosing "custom install", they are only needed if you want to use the tcltk R package or build package documentation from sources.

Note: the use of X11 (including tcltk) requires XQuartz to be installed since it is no longer part of OS X. Always re-install XQuartz when upgrading your macOS to a new major version.

This release supports Intel Macs, but it is also known to work using Rosetta2 on M1-based Macs. For native Apple silicon arm64 binary see below.

Important: this release uses Xcode 12.4 and GNU Fortran 8.2. If you wish to compile R packages from sources, you may need to download GNU Fortran 8.2 - see the tools directory.

R-4.1.2-arm64.pkg (notarized and signed)
SHA1-hash: 9bdf2f2fe29e7bfac826bfad63f82f0da94abedaa
(ca. 87MB)

R 4.1.2 binary for macOS 11 (**Big Sur**) and higher, **Apple silicon arm64** build, signed and notarized package. Contains R 4.1.2 framework, R.app GUI 1.77 for Apple silicon Macs (M1 and higher), Tcl/Tk 8.6.11 X11 libraries and Texinfo 6.7. **Important: this version does NOT work on older Intel-based Macs.**

Note: the use of X11 (including tcltk) requires XQuartz. Always re-install XQuartz when upgrading your macOS to a new major version.

This release uses Xcode 12.4 and experimental GNU Fortran 11 arm64 fork. If you wish to compile R packages from sources, you may need to download GNU Fortran for arm64 from https://mac.R-project.org/libs-arm64. Any external libraries and tools are expected to live in /opt/R/arm64 to not conflict with Intel-based software and this build will not use /usr/local to avoid such conflicts.

4. Now that you have downloaded the correct version of R for your system, all left is to open the downloaded installer files and let it run through its installation process.

Now I don't recommend using R in this form. It is just a simple text editor, and you may find it a bit difficult to use as a beginner. I will not recommend it for the beginner stage. Once you get comfortable with the code, you may use it, but not at this stage.

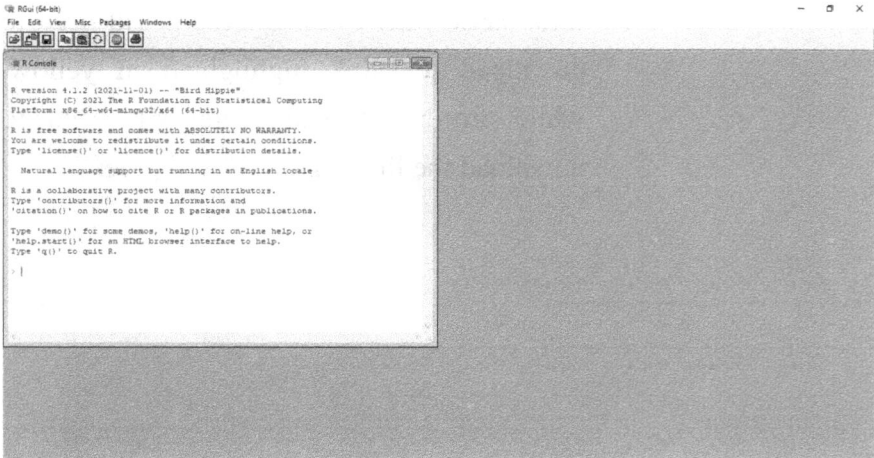

Instead, we will download and integrate the developer environment (IDE). There are many IDES available, but R is an open-source language, and you must use an open-source IDE such as RStudio. An IDE increases your level of overall productivity. RStudio remembers every detail about your work that you simply cannot remember. For instance, Compared to using just R, you have to remember the names of packages.

Choosing an integrated developer environment (IDE)

Why use an IDE?

An IDE has many useful features. Some of them are mentioned below

- It reduces the chance of error

- It manages your residual data. You don't have to clean up the intermediary files.

- RStudio has multiple panels to see numerous features on a single screen.

- It gives hints regarding your performance and refactoring.

- It allows you to inspect your code instantly.

- It gives a final result preview.

Now that you have R installed on your computer, you can input R commands and use the language as needed. While you are more than welcome to stop following this chapter here, this book greatly recommends using an integrated development environment (also known as an IDE). An IDE is software that acts as a graphical user inference for your R projects. Think of it as your web browser to R. Using an IDE makes for a more straightforward R session.

There are many different IDEs for R, and each comes with its advantages and disadvantages, but this book will be focusing exclusively on the use of RStudio. Again while RStudio is not specifically required to use R, for those with little-to-no programming experience, using RStudio will make following along with this ebook easier as many of the images shown will be of the RStudio environment.

Installing RStudio Desktop

As stated earlier, we will be using RStudio Desktop as our IDE of choice for this book. So whether you are using Windows, macOS, or Linux, Rstudio has an option for you. It is also worth noting that for those using a Chromebook or a system not supported by a

Desktop version of RStudio, there is also a lightweight free-to-use cloud-based version of Rstudio that can be accessed at https://www.rstudio.com/products/cloud/. For those of you who would like to follow along with RStudio Desktop, here are some instructions on installing the program to your system.

1. Much like installing R, installing RStudio is a quick and painless process. First, you will navigate to the "Rstudio download page" "(https://www.rstudio.com/products/rstudio/download/)," where you will be greeted with four different versions of RStudio Desktop. For this book and its most uses, the free open source license of Rstudio Desktop is an excellent choice.

2. After selecting which version of RStudio you would like to download, you will be taken to a download page where we could choose the proper "installer" for your "operating system"

RStudio Desktop 2021.09.1+372 - Release Notes

1. Install R. RStudio requires R 3.0.1+

2. Download RStudio Desktop. Recommended for your system:

DOWNLOAD RSTUDIO FOR WINDOWS
2021.09.1+372 | 156.89MB

Requires Windows 10 (64-bit)

All Installers

Linux users may need to import RStudio's public code-signing key prior to installation, depending on the operating system's security policy.

RStudio requires a 64-bit operating system. If you are on a 32 bit system, you can use an older version of RStudio.

OS	Download	Size	SHA-256
Windows 10	RStudio-2021.09.1-372.exe	156.89 MB	1d9327f5
macOS 10.14+	RStudio-2021.09.1-372.dmg	203.00 MB	0 aec0442
Ubuntu 18/Debian 10	rstudio-2021.09.1-372-amd64.deb	117.89 MB	92164223
Fedora 19/Red Hat 7	rstudio-2021.09.1-372-x86_64.rpm	133.83 MB	f1b43649
Fedora 28/Red Hat 8	rstudio-2021.09.1-372-x86_64.rpm	133.85 MB	ba2637c6
Debian 9	rstudio-2021.09.1-372-amd64.deb	118.10 MB	607cd445
OpenSUSE 15	rstudio-2021.09.1-372-x86_64.rpm	119.78 MB	472d028e

3. Once you have downloaded the installer that matches your operating system, the process is as easy as opening the downloaded installer file and allowing it to run through its installation. Once the installer has finished, you will be ready to use RStudio.

Chapter 2

Navigating Rstudio

Starting Concepts

R is launched by starting the relevant executable after it has been installed on your computer. R is waiting for your instructions, as shown by the prompt '>'. Some tasks (opening online assistance, opening files, etc.) may be done via the pull-down menus under Windows using the software Rgui.exe. A new user might be wondering, "What do I do now?" at this point. When using R for the first time, it is quite helpful to have a few concepts about how it works, and that is exactly what we will see now. First, let's have a look at how R works. Then I'll go through how to use the "assign" operator to create data, how to cope with data in system memory, and how we can use the online support, which is quite helpful when using R.

Introduction to the Interface of R

When opening Rstudio for the first time, you will be greeted with a screen that looks like this:

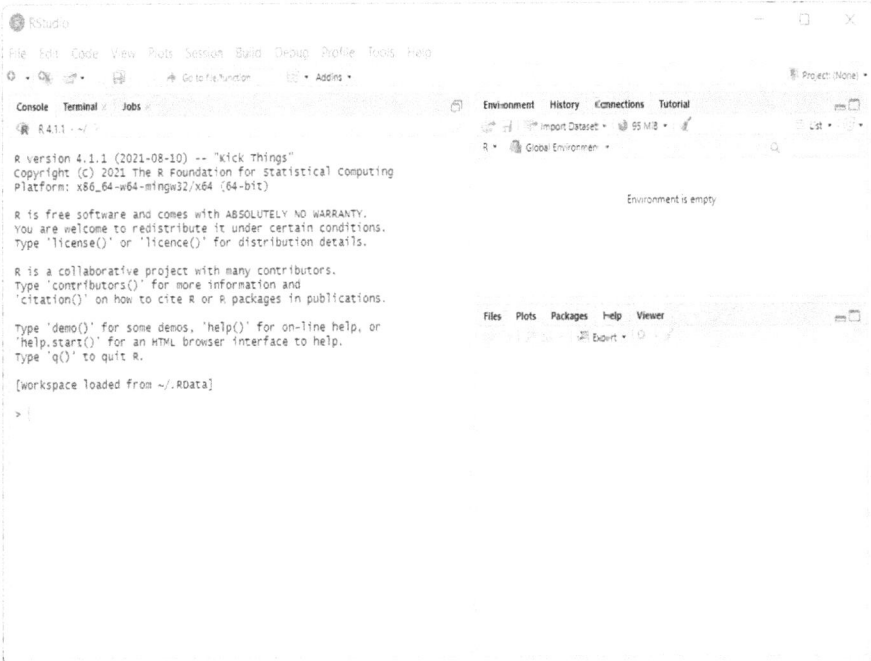

Here you can see a menu bar that has multiple tabs. Each tab has a drop-down menu itself to guide you through it.

In the menu bar, you will get a drop-down bar for each content, as you can see.

Most of them are self-explanatory.

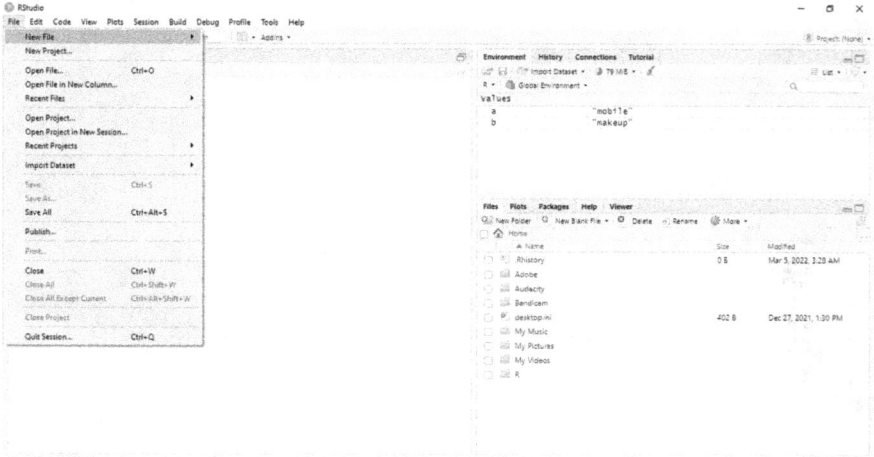

When you first open Rstudio, you will notice three separate panes, the Console, the Environment, and the Viewer panes.

The Console

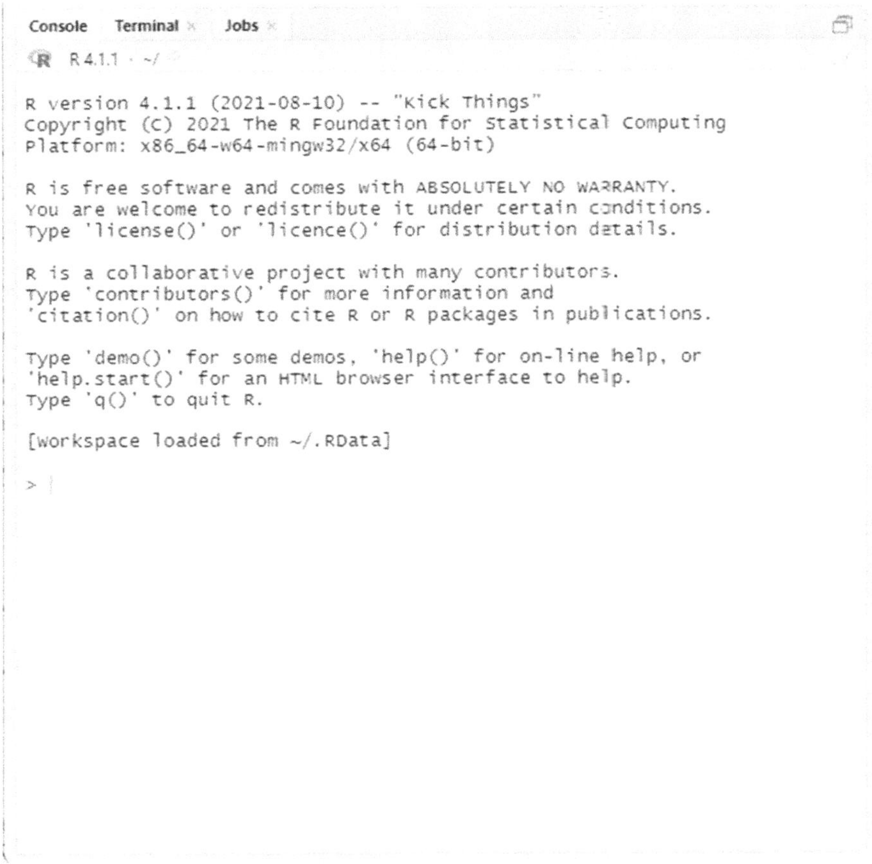

```
Console   Terminal    Jobs

R   R 4.1.1 · ~/

R version 4.1.1 (2021-08-10) -- "Kick Things"
Copyright (C) 2021 The R Foundation for Statistical Computing
Platform: x86_64-w64-mingw32/x64 (64-bit)

R is free software and comes with ABSOLUTELY NO WARRANTY.
You are welcome to redistribute it under certain conditions.
Type 'license()' or 'licence()' for distribution details.

R is a collaborative project with many contributors.
Type 'contributors()' for more information and
'citation()' on how to cite R or R packages in publications.

Type 'demo()' for some demos, 'help()' for on-line help, or
'help.start()' for an HTML browser interface to help.
Type 'q()' to quit R.

[workspace loaded from ~/.RData]

>
```

Seen on the leftmost side of the Rstudio window is the console. It can be argued that this is the single most important pane within RStudio, as it is where all of your code will run. If you ever wish to do so, you can even do everything you would like to do in R from the console alone.

The Environment Pane

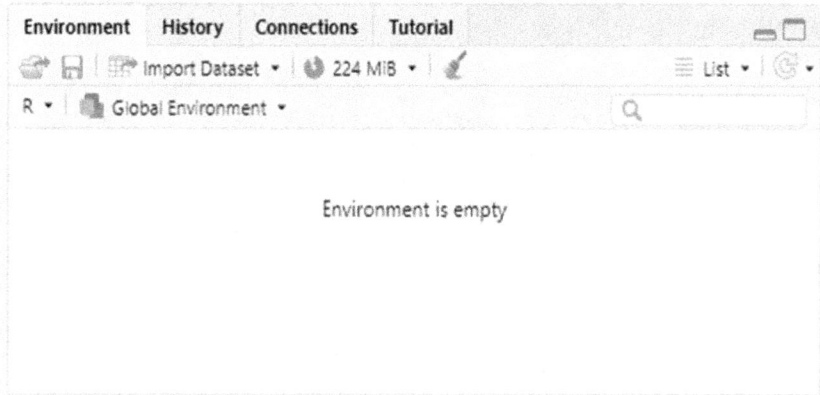

The Environment Pane will be found in the top right corner of the RStudio window. This area is where you will find the current objects within your Environment (also known as your workspace). These objects will include data frames, matrixes, functions, values, arrays, and more that you have created or added to your workspace. The Environment Pane will also serve as a convenient graphical user interface for some of the more mundane functions of R, such as View ().

The Environment pane also shares its space with three other common panes, which you can see at the top, called "History," "Connections," and "Tutorial." Within the History tab, you will find a record of all the commands run within your R session. The Connections tab is where you will be able to connect to and view data from an outside source, such as SQLServer, Salesforce, etc. Finally, the Tutorial tab will interact with the learner package if you so wish. This book will place nearly all of its emphasis on the Environment tab within this pane.

The Viewer Pane

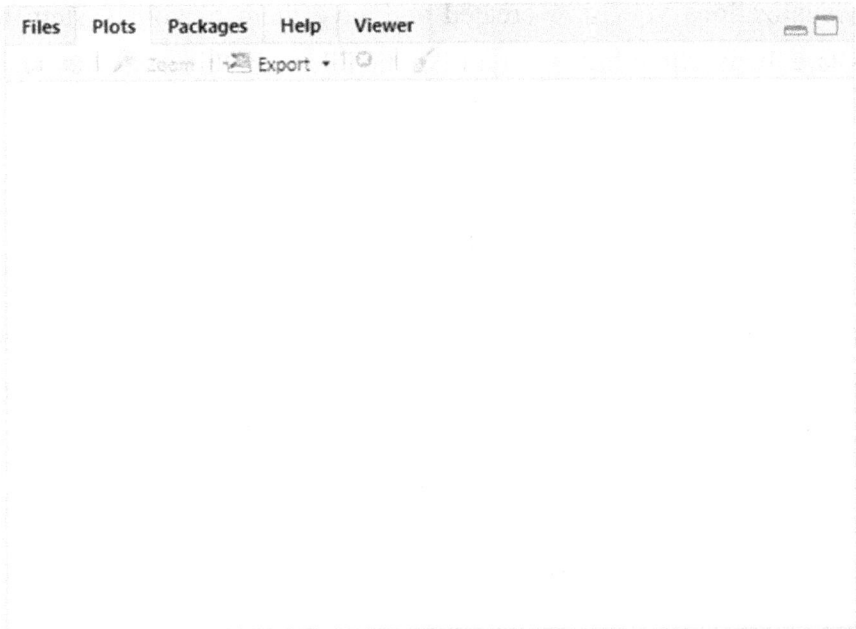

Files	Plots	Packages	Help	Viewer		

Finally, we come to the Viewer pane seen in the bottom right portion of the RStudio window. Like the Environment pane, the Viewer Pane shares its space with many other features. These are the "Files", "Plots", "Packages", "Help", and "Viewer tabs. Another similarity with the Environment pane is how these individual tabs act as easy-to-use graphical user interfaces for various functions of R.

The Files tab is an easy way to quickly see the files on your system and set the working directory, just like the file manager on your operating system. Acting as a point and click version of many R Functions such as setwd().

Next is the Plots tab. Here is where you will view any visualizations you have created and save them to your system to share them with others easily. Like the Files tab, this is another easy point and click interface that acts the same as executing R commands in the console.

The Packages tab is another convenient area where you can easily view and install common packages found within the CRAN by simply pointing your mouse and choosing which packages to install. Effectively acting as both the install.package() and library() functions. This is particularly helpful if you know what you are needed to accomplish but are not sure what package you need.

	Files	Plots	Packages	Help	Viewer		

	Name	Description	Version		
System Library					
✓	base	The R Base Package	4.1.1		
☐	boot	Bootstrap Functions (Originally by Angelo Canty for S)	1.3-28		
☐	class	Functions for Classification	7.3-19		
☐	cluster	"Finding Groups in Data": Cluster Analysis Extended Rousseeuw et al.	2.1.2		
☐	codetools	Code Analysis Tools for R	0.2-18		
☐	compiler	The R Compiler Package	4.1.1		
✓	datasets	The R Datasets Package	4.1.1		
☐	foreign	Read Data Stored by 'Minitab', 'S', 'SAS', 'SPSS', 'Stata', 'Systat', 'Weka', 'dBase', ...	0.8-81		
✓	graphics	The R Graphics Package	4.1.1		
✓	grDevices	The R Graphics Devices and Support for Colours and Fonts	4.1.1		
☐	grid	The Grid Graphics Package	4.1.1		

The Help tab is extremely useful when working with a new and unfamiliar function. In this tab, you access the CRAN R

Documentation pages to find descriptions and demonstrations of nearly all R functions. This can also be accessed by typing a ? in front of any function in the console. For example, if you would like to learn more about the setwd() function mentioned earlier, you could either go to the Help tab and search setwd or simply type ?setwd() into the console then hit the enter key to execute. Both methods will greet you with the information pictured below.

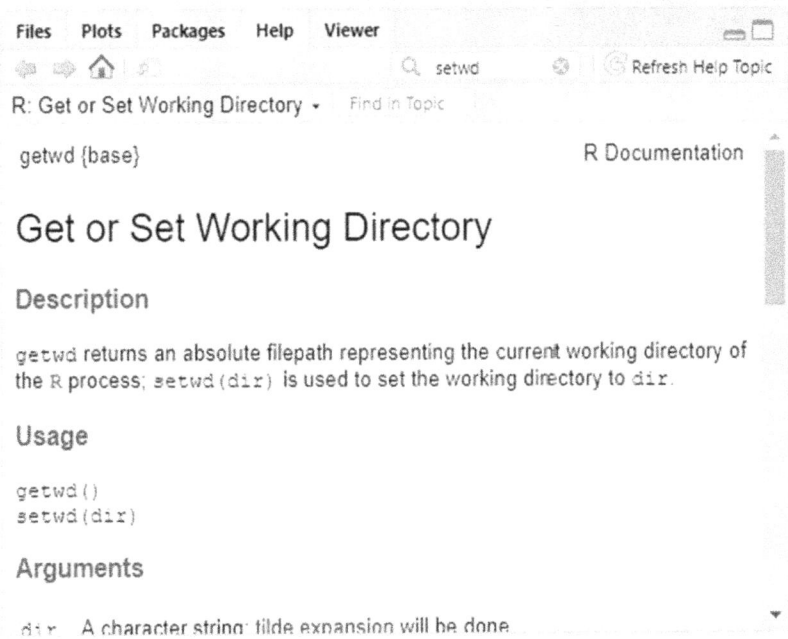

Files   Plots   Packages   Help   Viewer

R: Get or Set Working Directory ·   Find in Topic

getwd {base}   R Documentation

Get or Set Working Directory

Description

getwd returns an absolute filepath representing the current working directory of the R process; setwd(dir) is used to set the working directory to dir.

Usage

```
getwd()
setwd(dir)
```

Arguments

dir   A character string; tilde expansion will be done

Lastly is the Viewer tab. This tab can be used to view locally stored web content. You can use it to view locally stored HTML files or locally run applications.

This book will not place much weight on this tab as it is a more specialized tab that most users will not be using.

Source Pane

First, the first thing you need to do is open a new script. To do that, you will follow

File in the menu, new file, R Script.

After opening R Script, you will see a new console named source pan. Here you can practice your code first. As you can see, I already wrote a code here. It is very useful during practice and will save lots of your precious time.

You just have to select the required core line and hit run to execute the code. And it will transfer your code to the console pan, making them variables.

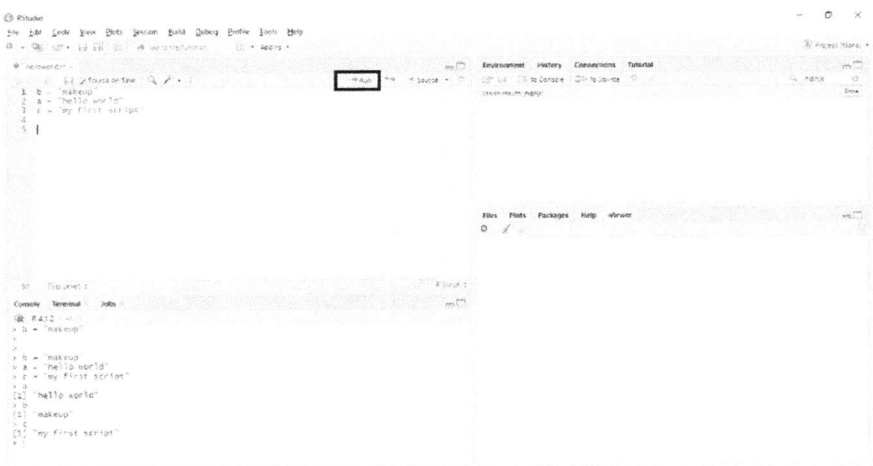

Chapter 3

Your First Lines of Code

Now that you have R installed and have gotten your IDE setup, it is finally time to begin writing your first lines of code. Before writing, you must know that when you save the file, you must use the .r or. R extension or it will not open next time in the r studio.

For those who have yet to have any experience in coding, let me first mention that coding is just like learning any other skill. While it may seem daunting at first, you will quickly find out that learning to code can be incredibly easy and fun with the proper guidance and practice. Without further delay, let us dig into RStudio and get comfortable writing our first lines of code.

Syntax

R is a case-sensitive language, and it is necessary to understand the difference between "eCommerce" and "eCommerce." When you complete this part of the book, you will differentiate between these two commands.

Statements: this is a programming language used for every task in R programming. The task or statement could be anything, such as adding two numbers together. Or multiply them, as you can see in the following picture.

In the first line, I assigned a variable. What is variable will be discussed separately.

In the second line, I simply print a line using a print statement, and in the last, I assign some values to statements a and b. Using the command statement, I multiplied both statements and got the answer.

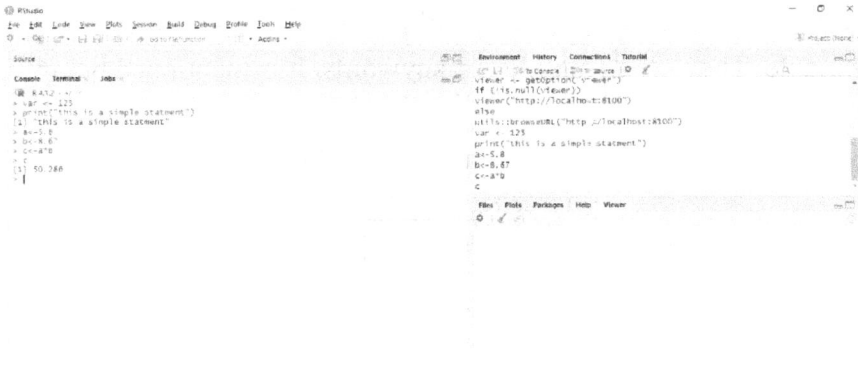

Comments: while writing a code, we usually add random comments to remember or describe a piece of code. You can also use a history pan for this purpose.

The comments may be a single line or multiple lines. The difference between them is that single liner comments often begin with a # sign, for example

#this is the single-line comment

And multiple liners are secured with, for example

"This is line one

And

This is line 2."

Keywords: keywords are reserved phrases that you cannot use as a variable. They are a small list of keywords. It is mentioned below.

If	For	FALSE
In	Else	NA_integer_
NA_real_	NULL	Next
Repeat	Inf	NA_complex_
While	NaN	NA
Function	Break	TRUE
NA_character_		

Write your first R Script

Here we will learn to print our first statement. It can be anything you want for the sake of learning. Normally the first script in any programming is "Hello World."

So using syntax as we discussed above will be

```
Print ("text")
```

```
Console   Terminal    Jobs
R  R 4.1.2  ~/
> print("hello world")
[1] "hello world"
>
```

Just like that, you printed your first statement. So far, you should write a statement and save it as we discussed before.

Types of Data

R program supports six types of data. Data can be of different kinds. For example, if you want to add someone's age along with their name. Age will be an integer, while the name will be a string. Other variables include Boolean values where you have to choose either YES or NO or TRUE or FALSE. The rest variables are in the following table.

Data type	Integer	Complex	Raw	Character	Numeric	logical
Example	0l, 888l, 878l	7+9i, -16+87i	The word awesome will be as 41 77 65 73 6f 6d 65	"dot", "don't", "hello"	7, 787, 76745 2366.88	True, FALSE
Explanations	Only for integer storing	Complex numbers with real and imaginary parts	Hexadecimal form of Values	For strings but must be enclosed with quotes.	Numeric or decimal values	Boolean values.

Variables

Variables are the names for the data storage location. The system reserved a small part when we declared a variable. If we avoid using variables, the address R assigned to our script is a hexadecimal address. You can never find those, as earlier, you saw an example of the hexadecimal form of the word "awesome." Assigning a variable to data makes it easy to remember the address of that data.

Another benefit of variables is that you do not need to worry about your data type as it figures it out itself. As you can see in the following picture, I assign some character, logical, and complex variable data first, then I print it, and then using class, I can know what type of data is stored in those variables.

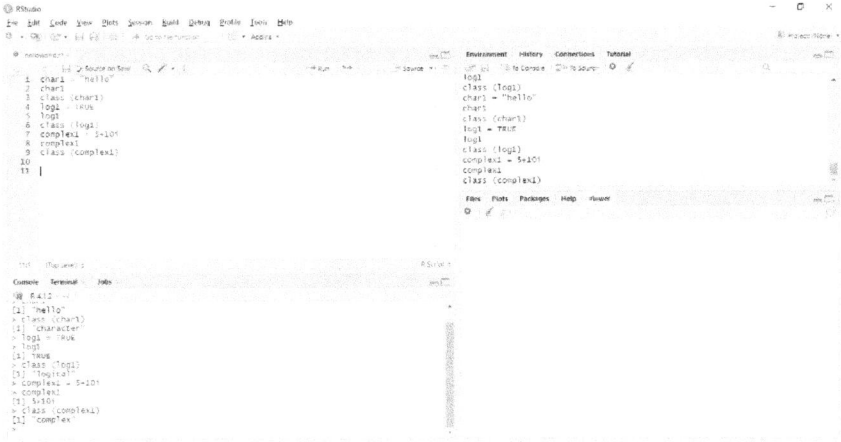

However, I will explain certain rules regarding naming your variable in detail.

1. You can use letters and numbers.

2. Only dot (.) and underscore (_) are allowed in the name of all the special characters.

3. you cannot start the name with a number or underscore

4. And the keywords that we discussed earlier are also not allowed.

Next, you need to learn how to assign data to a variable?

There are three operations in which you can assign data to your variable that are

- Equal to the operator (=)

- Leftwards operator (<-)

- Rightwards operator (->)

31

When using the equal to and leftward operators, the value is on the "right-hand side," and the variable is on the "left-hand side," resulting in a left-to-right assignment. The assignment is right to left when the variable is on the" right side," and the rightward operator is used with the value assigned on the" left side" For example, please see the following picture.

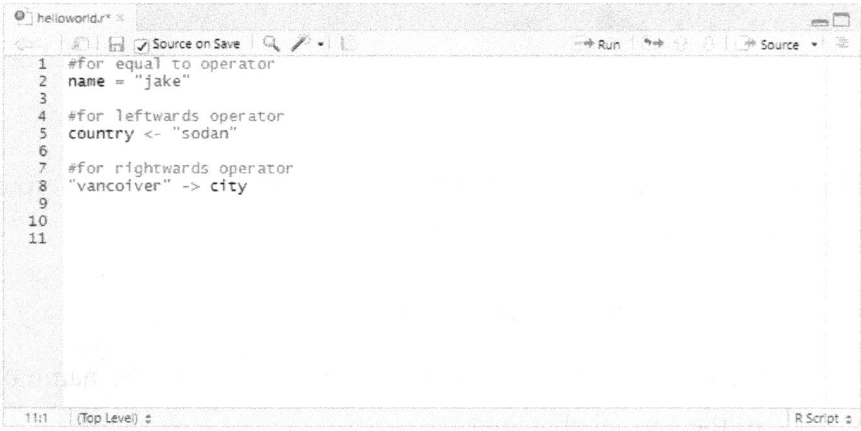

```
1  #for equal to operator
2  name = "jake"
3
4  #for leftwards operator
5  country <- "sodan"
6
7  #for rightwards operator
8  "vancoiver" -> city
9
10
11
```

Chapter 4

Operators and their types

An operator is a symbol or group of symbols that perform a computational task. A computational task can include

1. arithmetic

2. logical, and

3. relational operators

Among other things, We've already seen three different assignment operators for assigning values to variables. We'll learn more about other operators in this section.

Several operators are available in R, including arithmetic, logical, and assignment operators. Each of these categories will be discussed in depth.

A few operators don't fit into any categories and will be covered as needed. Because some operators work better with vectors, they'll be covered in the Vectors chapter.

Arithmetic operators:

For mathematics, we use arithmetic operators. These include,

Operator	Description	Sample Usage	Explanation
+	Addition	x + y	Adds the given operands, returns sum of the operands.
-	Subtraction	x - y	Subtracts the operand on the right from the one on the left, returns difference of the operands.
*	Multiplication	x * y	Multiplies operands and returns the product.
/	Division	x / y	Performs division and returns the quotient.
%%	Modulus	x %% y	Performs division and returns the remainder.
%/%	Integer Division	x %/% y	Performs, integer division and returns the quotient in integer form only. For example, if we divide 5 by 2, the quotient is 2.5. However, if we perform integer division like this --> 5 %/% 2, we will get the quotient as 2.
^	Exponent	x ^ y	Raises the power of the operand on the left by the operand on the right. For example, 2 ^ 5 will give us 32.

In the next picture, you will see how I perform simple mathematics in the r studio.

```
Console   Terminal    Jobs
R  R 4.1.2  ~/
> a = 2
> b = 10
> a
[1] 2
> a + b
[1] 12
> a * b
[1] 20
> a / b
[1] 0.2
> a %% b
[1] 2
> a ^ b
[1] 1024
>
```

I will explain it in detail here. With its design around statistics and data analysis, it is expected that R would be able to execute the same basic calculations as you would perform with a simple calculator. While this isn't the killer app of R, these basic calculations are vital to the more complex functions you will execute very soon. They will allow you to understand how a line of code is executed within the console.

Let's begin with the basic mathematical operators; addition, subtraction, multiplication, and division. We will begin with various equations of any numbers you would like. This book will be using the numbers 5 and 7. When performing our basic calculations, we must type the equation into the console and then hit enter to execute it. However, one key difference between running a calculation in R vs writing an equation on the chalkboard in class is that rather than typing in our equal sign, all we need to do is execute the calculation. Once executed, R will print your answer on the next line pictured below. Feel free to test this out with as many different combinations of numbers and operators to feel comfortable writing these basic commands.

```
>   5 + 7
[1]  12
>   5 + 7 + 5 / 7 * 5 - 3
[1]  12.57143
> 5 * 7
[1]  35
> 7 / 5
[1]  1.4
> 5 - 7
[1] -2
> (5 + 7) / 2
[1] 6
```

Let me sum up the things that we have learned so far. Now that you have a good understanding of how R can perform basic calculations let us further expand our knowledge by introducing objects. Much like a variable in algebra class in school, an object in R is simply a representation of another value. In other words, in the equation x = 57, "x" is an object that represents 57. Assigning values to objects in R is just as easy as writing that equation above.

Now, while R will recognize your assignment if you write your line of code as x = 57, it is generally considered bad form to do so. The reason for this is that when writing code, we will use the = symbol for more than just assigning values to objects. This is where the assignment operator comes in handy. In order to create an easier code that is easily read and understood, it is recommended that when assigning values to objects of any kind, you use the assignment operator <-. Regardless of what your goals are with programming in R, it's incredibly likely that you will be making a massive amount of assignments. Thankfully, <- if used in the same way as we would use =. Like the example above, we would create the same object result by typing x <- 57.

Unlike the traditional algebraic equation, our objects in R do not need their names to be restricted to single-character symbols and letters. In fact, oftentimes, you will find your code easier to read and understand if you use more descriptive names than the schoolhouse "X and Y." Not to mention that using "X and Y" as Object names could get confusing later on when coding graphical visualizations, considering we will use those letters to dictate axes for charts.

Objects themselves can be much more complex than simple integer values, and assigning names to objects is something you will find useful for many different kinds of objects, from vectors to data frames. You could even assign a name to one of the calculations you made earlier.

Try it yourself:

1. Execute an assignment like x <- 5 * 7 in the console. First, you will notice that by creating an object, RStudio has stored it within the environment tab, allowing you to see all the assignments you have made easily.

2. Now simply execute x in the console. You'll then see that R will print the result of your assignment in this book's example, that is 35.

Pro Tip, the developers of RStudio recognize the importance of assigning names to objects and have created a handy shortcut for the <- symbol. All you need to do is hit the Alt key and the - key together, and Rstudio will enter the <- symbol, including its surrounding spaces, into your line of code.

Understanding Functions

Now that you have an understanding of some of the calculations that R can perform and its ability to store objects for future use, it is important to get familiar with one of the most common elements you will encounter in R, the function. In R, a function is simply a predetermined set of instructions. In other words, to use the function "function_a()" you would simply type function_a(argument1, argument2) into the console.

Now, it is important to know that each function may require a different set of arguments, depending on what all the specific function needs in order to run. An argument is simply a piece of added instructions for the R function. Some arguments are required for a function, while some are optional.

Let's examine the function class(). The class function is a function that is used to determine the class of an object in R. At its most basic written form. It can simply look like a class("the object you want to know the class of"). You can test this with the object x you created earlier. By simply nesting x within the function and executing it in the console, R will quickly inform you of the x's object class. Try it out. Type class(x) into the console. Class() is an extremely useful function that you will no doubt use in your R programming journey.

```
> x <- 5 * 7
> x
[1] 35
> class(x)
[1] "numeric"
```

What is nice about programming in R is that many functions, regardless of whether they come from the base R or an installed package, follow this easy-to-understand syntax. While it is true that many functions require more than a single argument in order to run, once you understand what it is you are asking of R, it is easy to understand what arguments (or pieces) you need in order for the function to run properly. Just remember, if you ever need help understanding a function, you can simply type a ? in front of the function you need help with within the console, and the CRAN documentation will appear in the Viewer pane. For example, to learn more about the class function, you can execute: ?class() into the console.

You will have likely guessed that by the introduction of the class function, the classification of an object will prove to be very important when programming in R. Thankfully, however, the difference in the classes is relatively straightforward. This book will further explore the different classes of data in the next section regarding data structures.

Relational Operators

To compare operands, relational operators are used. Determine whether one operand is less than or greater than another, whether one operand is equal to another, and so on. TRUE or FALSE is returned by these operators. In R, 0 represents FALSE, while non-zero numbers, including negative numbers, represent TRUE. In control structures, relational operators are widely used. Please see the following picture.

Operator	Description	Sample Usage	Explanation
==	Equal To	x == y	Returns TRUE if the values of the operands are equal, FALSE otherwise.
!=	Not Equal To	x != y	Returns TRUE if the values of the operands are not equal, FALSE otherwise.
<	Less Than	x < y	Returns TRUE if the value of the left operand is less than the value of the operand on the right, FALSE otherwise.
>	Greater Than	x > y	Returns TRUE if the value of the left operand is greater than the value of the operand on the right, FALSE otherwise.
<=	Less Than OR Equal To	x <= y	Returns TRUE if the value of the left operand is less than *OR equal to* the value of the operand on the right, FALSE otherwise.
>=	Greater Than OR Equal To	x >= y	Returns TRUE if the value of the left operand is greater than *OR equal to* the value of the operand on the right, FALSE otherwise.

In the following picture, I will demonstrate the r script for the relational operator for your guidance. So as you can see in the following picture, I just assigned two values to variable x and variable y

And then, using relational operations, I simply ran the command script, and it started giving me data about the variables. Now here, I only assign two variables and a very small amount but imagine, if you have data in multiple variables, it will become so easy for you to gather your required information, and you will save so much time.

```
Console    Terminal    Jobs
R  R.4.1.2 · ~/
>  x  =  30
>  y  =  40
>  x  ==  b
[1] FALSE
>  x  !=  y
[1] TRUE
>  x<y
[1]  TRUE
>  x  <  y
[1]  TRUE
>  |
```

Logical Operators

The logical operators logical OR, AND, and NOT are used to perform logical operations. These operations produce either TRUE or FALSE as a result.

Operator	Description	Sample Usage	Explanation
||	Logical OR	x || y	Compares operands and returns TRUE if any one of the values is non-zero, returns FALSE otherwise .
&&	Logical AND	x && y	Compares operands and returns TRUE if all the values are non-zero, returns FALSE otherwise.
!	Logical NOT	!x	Returns inverted value of the operand in logical form. If the operand has a TRUE value (non-zero), FALSE will be returned and if the operand has a FALSE value (0), TRUE will be returned.

Elementwise OR (|) and Elementwise AND (&) are two variants of Logical OR and Logical AND. The only way to understand the differences between these variations is to use vectors, so they are covered in the Vectors chapter.

Here's a script to show you how to use logical operators:

41

```
Console    Terminal    Jobs
R  R 4.1.2 · ~/
> x=9
> y=-8
> a = TRUE
> b = FALSE
> x&&y
[1] TRUE
> !x
[1] FALSE
> !a
[1] FALSE
> !b
[1] TRUE
> a||b
[1] TRUE
> |
```

Data Structures

R's reliance on data and statistical analysis places heavy importance on the use of data structures. In the world of programming, you find the term data structure is used to describe a format for storing and organizing data. Those who have had experience using spreadsheet software will already have some experience with data structures, as a spreadsheet is simply a representation of one of the most common data structures you will encounter, known as a data frame.

Vectors

Another common type of data structure is a Vector. Simply put, a Vector is a group of various pieces of data that all share the same classification. Each column found within a "data frame" is a "Vector," and as such, every column in a "data frame" must also represent a single class of data. This book will focus primarily on the four most common types of Vector data classes found in data analysis: "Logical," "Integer," "Double," and "Character."

42

1. Logical vector data is a data type that represents a binary choice of data. Typically this is seen as TRUE/FALSE data.

2. Integer vector data is a numeric data type that represents only whole numbers. Such as 1, - 5, 101.

3. Double vector data is another numeric data type. However, unlike integer data, Double data represents fractional data in the form of decimals. Such as 105.1234

4. Character vector data is a data type that represents character strings. More easily put, character data is simply text. Such as, "Hello."

Creating a vector in R can be done very simply by exhausting the combined function. The combine function is found in base R that can be used to combine separate data points together into a singular vector as long as each data point is of the same class. The combine function is typed as c(). To create vectors with the combined function, all one needs to do is list each data point as a separate argument in the function.

Let us create a vector of each of the four data types discussed above by executing these lines of code into the console:

```
> logical_vector <- c(TRJE, TRUE,
FALSE, FALSE, FALSE)


> integer_vector <- c(10L, 36L, 8L,
```

```
        34L, 1L)
```

Note that in order to specify your numeric vector as integer data, you must type L at the end of each data point.

```
> double_vector <- c(4, 6, 4.12,
8.5, 2.23)


> character_vector <- c("Bart",
"Homer", "Lisa", "Marge", "Maggie")
```

Note each character data point is surrounded by quotations to inform R of the beginning and the end of each character string.

ou've just successfully created your very first vectors. Now try the class function on each of your vectors to see the data type of each one.

```
> class(logical_vector)
[1] "logical"
> class(integer_vector)
[1] "integer"
> class(double_vector)
[1] "numeric"
> class(character_vector)
[1] "character"
```

If using RStudio, you will also notice that these four vectors and some quick information about them, including their classes, can now be found in the environment pane.

Exponentials and log functions

Many times, we will read about scholars doing a "log" alteration on figures provided. This is the process of rescaling numbers using the logarithm.

The logarithm estimates the "power" that we have to raise the "base" to arrive at "x" when given a figure "X" and an observation called a "base."

The "log" of x = 340 to BASE 5 (transcribed arithmetically as) is an example. Log5 because $5^{3.6} = 340$, the answer is 3.6. The log transformation is accomplished in R.

Using the log function, we provide a log with the figure to convert, which is provided to you. As well as the base, which is allotted to the base?

The r script for the log is as follows:

1. Log(x=340,base=5)

2. The result would be 3.6

Here are a few things to think about:

- If x and its base both are +tive, the "LOG" of any amount "x = 1" when the "base= x."

- Regardless of the base, the log of x equals 1 is always 0.

The natural log is a type of LOG-transformation commonly used in mathematics that fixes the "base" at a certain arithmetical observation called "Euler's number." This is commonly abbreviated, for example, "e" and is about equivalent to "2.718".

The exp function is well-defined as an addition to the "power of x," where "x" could be some figure, which is derived from Euler's number (-tiv, 0, or +tiv).

The exp function "f(x) $=e^x$" is commonly abbreviated as "exp(x)," and it represents the opposite of the "natural log" with "exp($log_e x = log_e$ exp(x) = x"

The script which we will use in r for the exp function is as follows.

```
exp(x=5)
      The result would be: 148.4132
```

If we wish to use a value other than 'e', you have to supply the figures for the base. We included log and exp functions here because these functions are used later in the book. Most algebraic processes rely on them due to their numerous mathematical advantages.

Matrixes

You've mastered the use of vectors in R by now. A matrix is nothing more than a collection of vectors. A vector's size is determined by its length, but a matrix's size is determined by the number of rows and columns. Arrays, which are higher-dimensional structures, can also be created.

You'll start by observing how you can learn matrixes in r-language in the following chapter.

The matrix is a fundamental mathematical construct that is used in a variety of statistical procedures. A matrix A is commonly referred to as an m n matrix, meaning it has precisely X rows and Y columns. This indicates that I will contain m*n entrances, per item an "i," "j" with their distinctive location determined by the row "Q = 1, 2, y" and the column "(P = 1, 2, X)" To make a matrix in R, we can use matrix-function and pass the figures of a matrix as a vector to the data-argument:

```
RStudio
File  Edit  Code  View  Plots  Session  Build  Debug  Profile  Tools  Help

    Untitled1*      helloworld*     Untitled2*      Untitled3*
         Source on Save                                              Run         Source
    1   matr <- matrix(data=c(23,22,21,24,25,26), nrow = 3, ncol = 3)
    2   print(matr)
    3
    4

  3:1   (Top Level)                                                  R Script
Console  Terminal  Jobs
   R 4.1.2  ~/
>
> print(matr)
      [,1] [,2] [,3]
[1,]   23   24   23
[2,]   22   25   22
[3,]   21   26   21
>
```

To make a "matrix" in 'R,' we can practice with the "MATRIX-function" and pass the components of the "MATRIX" as a vector to

47

the 'DATA-argument' for example, I used the following script to create the example shown in the above picture.

```
matr <- matrix(data=c(23,22,21,24,25,26),
nrow = 3, ncol = 3)
print(matr)
```

You must ensure that the area between these vectors corresponds to the appropriate no. of rows (n row) &columns (n col). If we don't give nrow and ncol when calling matrix, R will return a single-column matrix containing the data elements as a default.

```
Matrix(data=c(23,22,21,24,25,26)
For example, is the same as
matrix(data=c(23,22,21,24,25,26),nrow=6,ncol
=1).
```

Selecting directions

It's crucial to understand how R populates the matrix with data entries. When viewing the data entries from left to right, we can see that the "2x2" matrices ("A") have been filled "column-by-column" in the preceding example. The parameter byrow can be used to influence how R fills in data, as seen in the following examples:

RStudio

File   Edit   Code   View   Plots   Session   Build   Debug   Profile   Tools   Help

○   ▾ ◎▾   ⟳▾   ⊟ ⊞   ⊞   ➷ Go to file/function   ⊞ ▾ Addins ▾

```
1   matr <- matrix(data=c(23,22,21,24,25,26), nrow = 3, ncol = 3)
2   print(matr)
3
4   matrix(data = c(23,22,21,24,25,26), nrow = 2, ncol=3,
5           byrow = FALSE)
6   |
```

6:1   (Top Level) ≑   R Script ≑

Console   **Terminal**   **Jobs**

```
R  R 4.1.2 · ~/
> matrix(data = c(23,22,21,24,25,26), nrow = 2, ncol=3,
+         byrow = FALSE)
     [,1] [,2] [,3]
[1,]   23   21   25
[2,]   22   24   26
> |
```

In this case, we've asked R to generate a 2X3 matrix containing the numbers (23,22,21,24,25,26). By setting the optional parameter byrow to FALSE, you instruct R to fill this 2x3 structure column-by-column, filling every column before going on to the next and interpreting the.'

"data-argument" value from the "left-hand side" to the "right-hand side." "R's" treatment of the "matrix" command is by-row=FALSE;

thus, if the by-row parameter isn't specified, the program assumes by-row=FALSE.

This behavior is seen in the above picture.

Similarly, if you set the parameter byrow to true, you instruct r to full this 2x3 structure row-by-row, and the result would be something like this:

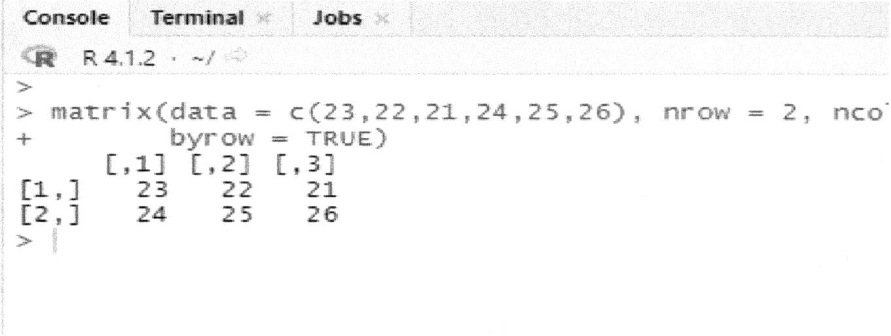

```
Console    Terminal ×    Jobs ×
R    R 4.1.2 · ~/
>
> matrix(data = c(23,22,21,24,25,26), nrow = 2, nco
+            byrow = TRUE)
       [,1]  [,2]  [,3]
[1,]    23    22    21
[2,]    24    25    26
>
```

Now, the data is being filled row by row.

Matrix bindings

If you have many equal length vectors, we can easily construct a matrix by binding them with the integrated R-functions c bind and r bind. We may either consider each vector either a row or a column (using the function r bind or c bind). Let's assume you have the 1:3, 4:6, and 7:9 vectors. The 2 3 matrices in the following picture may be reconstructed using rbind as follows:

```
2:1    (Top Level) ↕

Console   Terminal ×   Jobs ×
 R  R 4.1.2 · ~/
> rbind(1:3,4:6,7:9)
      [,1] [,2] [,3]
[1,]    1    2    3
[2,]    4    5    6
[3,]    7    8    9
>
```

Keep in mind, that if you want to use this function, the length of the vector should be identical.

The vectors have been tied together as 2-rows of the matrix by r bind, with the rows thoroughly in order to match the order of the vectors submitted to r bind. Using c bind, the matrix will be created as in the following example.

```
Console   Terminal ×   Jobs ×
 R  R 4.1.2 · ~/
> cbind(1:3,4:6,7:9)
      [,1] [,2] [,3]
[1,]    1    4    7
[2,]    2    5    8
[3,]    3    6    9
>
```

51

You have three vectors, each with a length of 2. You write these 3 vectors together in the command they were provided using cbind, and each vector develops a column in the final matrix.

The Matrix in Algebraic Operations

Matrixes may be seen from two views in R., To begin with, you can only use these as a calculation instrument in encoding to stock and alter outcomes, as you've seen. Otherwise, we may practice matrixes for arithmetic properties in relevant computations, similarly, matrix multiplication to describe "regression" model equations. This difference is essential since the arithmetic behavior of matrixes is not always the same as the more basic data management behavior. In this part, I'll go through some of the most mutual matrix-related arithmetic operations and their R equivalents, as well as some of the most unusual matrixes. You can avoid this section if you wish and get back to it later if you aren't interested in the mathematical behavior of matrixes. Transpose:

The nXm matrix formed through putting also replacing columns with rows or its rows with columns is the transpose, A^T, of any m × n matrix A^T.

Here's an illustration:

$$\text{If } A = \begin{matrix} 4 & 6 & 8 \\ 10 & 12 & 14 \end{matrix}, \text{ then } A^T = \begin{matrix} 4 & 10 \\ 6 & 12 \\ 8 & 14 \end{matrix}$$

In Rstudio, the transpose function is associated with *"t"* in the next example, I will illustrate how to make to utilize this function in R.

```
     Source on Save
1   x <- rbind(c(4,6,8), c(10,12,14))
2   x
3   t(x)
4   |
5
6
```

4:1   (Top Level) ‡

Console   **Terminal** ×   **Jobs** ×

R R 4.1.2 · ~/

```
> x
     [,1] [,2] [,3]
[1,]    4    6    8
[2,]   10   12   14
> t(x)
     [,1] [,2]
[1,]    4   10
[2,]    6   12
[3,]    8   14
>
```

Addition and Multiplication of Matrixes

A single, univariate value is referred to as a scalar value. Any figure, let's say A, multiplied by a scalar value produces a matrix where each independent section is multiplied by a.

As you can see, R does this multiplication element-by-element.

For example, lets multiply our previous equation, $\begin{matrix} 4 & 6 & 8 \\ 10 & 12 & 14 \end{matrix}$, with 3.

```
1  x <- rbind(c(4,6,8), c(10,12,14))
2  x
3  t(x)
4  a <- 3
5  a*x
6
```

6:1   (Top Level) ÷

Console   Terminal ×   Jobs ×

R   R 4.1.2 · ~/

```
> x
     [,1] [,2] [,3]
[1,]    4    6    8
[2,]   10   12   14
> t(x)
     [,1] [,2]
[1,]    4   10
[2,]    6   12
[3,]    8   14
> a <- 3
> a*x
     [,1] [,2] [,3]
[1,]   12   18   24
[2,]   30   36   42
>
```

As one could anticipate, The standard arithmetic * operator is used to perform scalar multiplication on a matrix.

Similarly, the element-wise + or - of 2 matrixes of identical size is also accomplished. Depending on the procedure, corresponding items are added or deleted from one another. For this, first, we need to create two elements named X and Y and assign them values using cbind or rbind.

```
⊕  ▾  ⦾ℝ  ⇦ ▾  🖫 🖫  ▤  ⇾  Go to file/function          ▯

  ⊚ Untitled1* ×   ⊚ helloworld.r ×   ⊚ kjkij.R ×   ⊚ Untitled3*

  ⇦    ℰ   🖫  ☐ Source on Save   🔍 🖉  ▾
  1   x <- rbind(c(4,6,8),  c(10,12,14))
  2   y<- rbind(c(1,2,3),c(7,8,9))
  3   x+y
  4   x-y
  5   x*y
  6   x/y
  7

  7:1      (Top Level) ⇕

  Console   Terminal ×   Jobs ×

  ℝ  R 4.1.2 · ~/
  > x+y
        [,1] [,2] [,3]
  [1,]    5    8   11
  [2,]   17   20   23
  > x-y
        [,1] [,2] [,3]
  [1,]    3    4    5
  [2,]    3    4    5
  > x*y
        [,1] [,2] [,3]
  [1,]    4   12   24
  [2,]   70   96  126
  > x/y
            [,1] [,2]     [,3]
  [1,] 4.000000  3.0 2.666667
  [2,] 1.428571  1.5 1.555556
  >
```

The + and - symbols can be used to add or remove any two
matrixes of equal size. It must be true that n = p to do multiplication
and divide 2 matrixes X and Y of sizes mXn and pXq. The size of
the resulting matrix Y X will be m q. The product's components are
computed row by row, with the rate at location (AB)i, j calculated
by component-wise multiplying the positioned values in a "row I of
X" by the positioned values in "column j of Y," then adding to the
outcome.

Multiplication of sufficiently sized matrixes (represented, for example, with C and D) is not interchangeable in general; that is, CXD, DXC.

Matrix multiplication, apart from +, -, and scalar multiplication, isn't a straightforward element-by-element calculation; hence we cannot use the ordinary * or (x) operator. In its place, we should use "R's matrix product operator", which is expressed as per cent * per cent in per cent symbols.

Chapter 5

Statistics in R

The process in which we convert data into information is called statistics. In order to find patterns and comprehend demographic characteristics. This chapter will go over some fundamental concepts and show how they may be applied using R.

Raw Data

Raw data, or the records that create a sample, is frequently the first item statistical analysts encounter. These data are saved in a specific R object, such as a data frame (Chapter 8), depending on the nature of the planned study. However, before you can start summarizing or modeling your data, you must first identify your accessible variables.

A variable is a property of a person in a group whose price varies among entities within that population. We tested with an illustrated "data frame" called "mydata" earlier, for example.

We took notes on the age, gender, and amount of humor of a group of individuals. These qualities are your variables, and the figures you measure are going to vary from man to man.

Variables could undertake a variety of shapes, dependent on the kind of values they can hold. You'll look at several conventional ways of describing variables before diving into R.

Numeric Data

The observations of a numeric variable are naturally recorded as numbers. Continuous and discrete numeric variables are the two types of numeric variables.

One **"continuous variable"** may document as "any value" in "any interval", up to some fractions (giving an unlimited amount of potential values, although the continuum is limited in series). If we were measuring rainfall, for example, a number of 17 mm would be reasonable, but so would a figure of 17.24135 mm. A valid observation can be made with any level of measurement precision.

A discrete random variable, however, can only engage different numeric figures, and the number of potential values is finite if the range is confined. Only whole numbers would make sense if we were totaling the no. of heads in 30 coin flips, for example. It's pointless to count 25.42135 heads since the potential results are limited to numbers from 0 to 30.

Category of variables

Although numeric observations are prevalent for many variables, categorical variables should also be considered. Categorical variables, like discrete variables, can only accept one of a limited number of options. Categorical observations, far from discrete variables, will not necessarily record as numeric figures.

Categorical variables are divided into two categories. Nominal objects are those that cannot be rationally ranked. Sex is an excellent example of a categorical-nominal variable. It has two fixed potential values in most data sets, female and male, and the categories of these data sets are immaterial. Ordinal variables are categorical variables that could be organically sorted. A pharmacological dose, for example, is a categorical, ordinal variable with three potential values high, low, and medium. These numbers could be arranged in rising or declining orders, and the order may be significant to the study.

For instance

Many statistics literature mix up the terms categorical and discrete variables when using them conversely. As this isn't always a bad idea, we like the definitions distinct enough for the purpose of clarity. We'll say, That is "discrete" once stating to a logically "numeric variable" e can not be stated on a "continuous scale" (like a total), and "categorical" as the likely results for a specific entity isn't always numeric, and the no. of alternative figures are always limited.

59

We can simply identify the types of variables in the data provided. Suppose you know what to look for. Take, for example, the *quakes* data frame from the automatically loaded datasets package. Directly putting the following at the prompt will give you the first five records of this data collection.

```
1
2   quakes[1:5,]
3   |
```

3:1   (Top Level) ≑

Console   **Terminal** ×   **Jobs** ×

R R 4.1.2 · ~/

```
> quakes[1:5,]
     lat    long depth mag stations
1 -20.42 181.62   562 4.8       41
2 -20.62 181.03   650 4.2       15
3 -26.00 184.10    42 5.4       43
4 -17.97 181.66   626 4.1       19
5 -20.42 181.96   649 4.0       11
> |
```

These data are described in R's help file *(quakes)* as the location of 1000 seismic events near Fiji. Let's read the five columns as vectors in their entireness:

Uni and Multi-variation of Data:

Data that is univariate and multivariate

You're working with univariate data when you're talking about or analyzing data that only has one dimension. Let's say a new data set named "chickwts" has The weight variable, as an example, is uni variate because every measurement can be described using only a single integer.

```
                      Source on Save                                          Run              Source
   1   chickwts$weight
   2   chickwts$feed
   3

1:1    (Top Level)                                                                                    R Scrip

Console   Terminal    Jobs

R  R 4.1.2  ~/
> chickwts$weight
 [1] 179 160 136 227 217 168 108 124 143 140 309 229 181 141 260 203 148 169 213 257 244
[22] 271 243 230 248 327 329 250 193 271 316 267 199 171 158 248 423 340 392 339 341 226
[43] 320 295 334 322 297 318 325 257 303 315 380 153 263 242 206 344 258 368 390 379 260
[64] 404 318 352 359 216 222 283 332
> chickwts$feed
 [1] horsebean horsebean horsebean horsebean horsebean horsebean horsebean horsebean
 [9] horsebean horsebean linseed   linseed   linseed   linseed   linseed   linseed
[17] linseed   linseed   linseed   linseed   linseed   linseed   soybean   soybean
[25] soybean   soybean   soybean   soybean   soybean   soybean   soybean   soybean
[33] soybean   soybean   soybean   soybean   sunflower sunflower sunflower sunflower
[41] sunflower sunflower sunflower sunflower sunflower sunflower sunflower sunflower
[49] meatmeal  meatmeal  meatmeal  meatmeal  meatmeal  meatmeal  meatmeal  meatmeal
[57] meatmeal  meatmeal  meatmeal  casein    casein    casein    casein    casein
[65] casein    casein    casein    casein    casein    casein    casein
Levels: casein horsebean linseed meatmeal soybean sunflower
>
```

Your data is termed multivariate when it is essential to include variables that are in multi-dimensions. When the different components of a statistical study aren't as valuable when analyzed separately (in other words, as univariate numbers), multivariate measures are perhaps the most important.

Spatial coordinates, for example, must be thought of in terms of not less than 2 components—a horizontal and a vertical component. The x-axis values alone aren't particularly helpful as univariate data. Consider the previous example of quakes data set, which comprises results on "1,000 seismic incidences" documented off the coast of "Fiji." You can rapidly gain a decent sense of what's displayed if you read the first 5 archives and see the explanations in the help file/chickwts of file/"quakes."

values
| a | 3 |
| data type | chr [1:5] NA "integer" "logical" NA "character |

Files Plots Packages Help Viewer

chickwts

R: Chicken Weights by Feed Type ▾   file?chickwts   < >

chickwts {datasets}   R Documentation

Chicken Weights by Feed Type

Description

An experiment was conducted to measure and compare the effectiveness of various feed supplements on the growth rate of chickens.

Usage

```
chickwts
```

Format

| a | 3 |
| data type | chr [1:5] NA "integer" "logical" NA "character" |

Files Plots Packages Help Viewer

quakes

R: Locations of Earthquakes off Fiji ▾   file?chickwts   < >

quakes {datasets}   R Documentation

Locations of Earthquakes off Fiji

Description

The data set give the locations of 1000 seismic events of MB > 4.0. The events occurred in a cube near Fiji since 1964.

Usage

```
quakes
```

Format

Is it a parameter or a statistic?

As previously said, statistics is concerned with comprehending the characteristics of a whole population, which is known as the complete group of persons or things of concern. The population's features are called parameters. Scholars often select a example of individuals toward exemplify the "population" and collect related "data" from these individuals since they seldom have access to related data on each member of the population of concern. They may then use the "sample data" to evaluate the parameters of interest, and those approximations are the statistics.

In particular, if you were ordered to gather data on ladies who own cat/dog in the United States, the "population of interest" will be all ladies who live in the "United States" and has one or more than one cat/dog. The honest mean age of those ladies living in "the United States" who have one or more than one cat/dog is the parameter of interest. Finding the age of every single woman in America who has a cat/dog would, of course, be a daunting task. A more real way will be to select a minor group of cat/dog-owning American ladies at random and collect information from the ladies, this would be our "sample," and the "mean-age" of the ladies in the taster will be our data for the statistic.

The main distinction between the parameter and the statistics is if the feature applies to the trial model you used or the whole population. The mean of a quantity for entities in a population is the framework, and the "mean x" of a taster of entities is the statistic element.

Basic Statistics

We're ready to compute some basic statistics with R now that we've learnt till now. In this part, you'll learn about the most common statistical methods for summarising the many sorts of variables I've covered.

Mean, median, and mode

Centrality measures are frequently used to describe huge datasets by specifying where numeric observations are centered. The arithmetic mean is, of course, one of the most popular measurements of centrality. It's said to be the 'center of gravity" of a collection of observations.

$$\bar{x} = \frac{(x_1 + x_2 + x_3 + \cdots \ldots x_n)}{n} = \frac{1}{n} \sum_{i=1}^{n} x_i \text{ for example,}$$

$$\bar{x} = \frac{2 + 5 + 6 + 11 + 11 + 44 + 24 + 51}{8} = 19.25$$

If you rank your data from minimum to biggest, we can calculate the median by selecting the central value (if the observations are not even) or by calculating the sum of the 2 central values (if the observations are even).

Sorting the data from smallest to largest produces 2,5,6,11,24,44,51,66 You have n/2 = 4 with n = 8 observations. As a result, the median is as follows:

$$(x_i^{(4)} + x_j^5) \div 2 = (11 + 11) \div 2 = 11$$

Simply said, the most repeated number is called mode as it is the "most common" observation. This statistic does not employ numeric-continuous data and is more usually employed with numeric-discrete data; however, it is sometimes used in relation to interims of the latter (for example, while discussing probability density functions in Elementary Statistics. a set of X measurements x1, x2,..., xn can have no mode (i.e., each figure is exceptional) or many modes (i.e., each figure is diverse) Just organize the frequency of the measurements to obtain the mode d x.

The frequencies may be shown here using the eight observations from the previous example:

Values	2	5	6	11	44	24	51
freq	1	1	1	2	1	1	1

The value 11 appears twice, which is more than any other value; hence the value 11 is the sole model for this data.

The arithmetic mean and median are straightforward to compute in R using built-in functions with the same names. To begin, create the numeric vector xdata from the eight observations.

Using R's table function to get the frequencies you need is probably the easiest way to find a mode.

```
titled1* ×      ● helloworld.r ×      ● kjkij.R ×      ● Untitle

            ⬚    ☐ Source on Save   🔍 ✏ ▾
    1   x<- c(2,5,6,11,11,44,24,51)
    2   mean(x)
    3   m.bar <- median(x)
    4   m.bar
    5   xtab <- table(x)
    6   xtab
    7

    7:1     (Top Level) ⬍

 Console   Terminal ×   Jobs ×

 ℝ  R 4.1.2 · ~/
 > x<- c(2,5,6,11,11,44,24,51)
 > mean(x)
 [1] 19.25
 > m.bar <- median(x)
 > m.bar
 [1] 11
 > xtab <- table(x)
 > xtab
 x
  2   5   6 11 24 44 51
  1   1   1  2  1  1  1
 >
```

The above example clearly displays the most repeated observation
for a tiny data set, known as mode; writing code that can
automatically determine the most common figure or data for any
table is a good practice. The smallest and greatest values are
reported by the min and max functions, respectively, with the range
returning both in a 2-dimensional vector.

titled1* × | helloworld.r × | kjklj.R × | Untitled3* × | Untitled4* × | »

```
      Source on Save   Q  /  ▾          → Run   →  ⤷ Source  ▾
  3   m.bar <- median(x)
  4   m.bar
  5   xtab <- table(x)
  6   xtab
  7   min(x)
  8   max(x)
  9   range(x)
 10
```

10:1   (Top Level) ‡   R Scr

Console   Terminal ×   Jobs ×

```
R  R 4.1.2 · ~/
> x<- c(2,5,6,11,11,44,24,51)
> mean(x)
[1] 19.25
> m.bar <- median(x)
> m.bar
[1] 11
> xtab <- table(x)
> xtab
x
 2  5  6 11 24 44 51
 1  1  1  2  1  1  1
> min(x)
[1] 2
> max(x)
[1] 51
> range(x)
[1]  2 51
>
```

Let's go back to the chickwts data set that we looked at previously.

The following are the chicks' mean and median weights:

```
Source on Save                                    Run        Source
1  chickwts$weight
2  chickwts$feed
3  mean(chickwts$weight)
4  median(chickwts$weight)
```

```
4:24   (Top Level) ¢                                                          R S
Console   Terminal   Jobs
R   R 4.1.2 · ~/
> chickwts$weight
 [1] 179 160 136 227 217 168 108 124 143 140 309 229 181 141 260 203 148 169 213 257 244
[22] 271 243 230 248 327 329 250 193 271 316 267 199 171 158 248 423 340 392 339 341 226
[43] 320 295 334 322 297 318 325 257 303 315 380 153 263 242 206 344 258 368 390 379 260
[64] 404 318 352 359 216 222 283 332
> chickwts$feed
 [1] horsebean horsebean horsebean horsebean horsebean horsebean horsebean horsebean
 [9] horsebean horsebean linseed   linseed   linseed   linseed   linseed   linseed
[17] linseed   linseed   linseed   linseed   linseed   linseed   soybean   soybean
[25] soybean   soybean   soybean   soybean   soybean   soybean   soybean   soybean
[33] soybean   soybean   soybean   soybean   sunflower sunflower sunflower sunflower
[41] sunflower sunflower sunflower sunflower sunflower sunflower sunflower sunflower
[49] meatmeal  meatmeal  meatmeal  meatmeal  meatmeal  meatmeal  meatmeal  meatmeal
[57] meatmeal  meatmeal  meatmeal  casein    casein    casein    casein    casein
[65] casein    casein    casein    casein    casein    casein    casein
Levels: casein horsebean linseed meatmeal soybean sunflower
> mean(chickwts$weight)
[1] 261.3099
> median(chickwts$weight)
[1] 258
>
```

You may also look at the quakes data set that was previously discussed. The following is the most repeated magnitude in the data set for earthquakes, indicating that there were 107 instances of a 4.5 magnitude event:

```
1   tab<- table(quakes$mag)
2   tab
3   tab[tab==max(tab)]
4
```

4:1   (Top Level) ⇕   R Script

Console   Terminal ×   Jobs ×

R R 4.1.2 · ~/
> tab<- table(quakes$mag)
> tab

  4 4.1 4.2 4.3 4.4 4.5 4.6 4.7 4.8 4.9   5 5.1 5.2
 46 55 90 85 101 107 101 98 65 54 47 43 29
5.3 5.4 5.5 5.6 5.7 5.9   6 6.1 6.4
 21 20 14   9   8   2   3   1   1
> tab[tab==max(tab)]
4.5
107
> |

For most practical uses, there are several ways of computing medians; however, the influence on outcomes is typically small. I've just used R's default "sample" version in this case.

Finally, remember that the tapply function is used to generate statistics aggregated by a specified category variable when generating basic summary statistics. Let's say we are asked to gather data that indicates the mean weight of chickens classified by their type of feed. The mean function in R is the most suitable option for each individual subgroup.

70

```
1  mean(chickwts$weight[chickwts$feed=="linseed"])
2  |
```

```
2:1   (Top Level) ÷                                        R Script :
```

```
Console  Terminal   Jobs

R  R 4.1.2 · ~/
> mean(chickwts$weight[chickwts$feed=="linseed"])
[1] 218.75
>
```

Non-numeric data

The data provided in R for chickens in the form of "chickwts" is not always numerical. It's useless to request "R" to calculate "mean of the variable" categorically, none the less counting the no. of observations that drop into each group is occasionally useful—these frequencies are the most basic summary statistic data for each category.

This can be used for the same count summary when calculating mode, so we can use the table function to get frequencies once more. The food of the chickens in the "chickwts" data set is made up of six different feed kinds. It's as simple as this to get these factor-level sums.

```
1  table(chickwts$feed)
2
```

```
> table(chickwts$feed)

   casein horsebean    linseed  meatmeal   soybean
       12        10         12        11        14
sunflower
       12
>
```

Via determining the parts of observations that drop into every group respectively, you may glean more information from these counts. This will provide you with measurements that are comparable across many data sets. The fraction of observations in each category is represented by proportions, which are commonly written as a scientific notation that lies between "0 and 1". To determine proportions, just divide the frequencies by the total sample size.

```
  ⊙ Untitled4* ⊗    ⊙ kjkj.R ⊗    ⊙ Untitled3* ⊗    ⊙ Untitled5* ⊗    »  ▬□
        ⌐  ⊟ ☐ Source on Save  Q  ⁄ ▾  [   →  ⤴  ⤻ Source ▾  ☰
   1   table(chickwts$feed)/nrow(chickwts)
   2  |
   3

  2:1    (Top Level) ⬥                                              R Script ⬥

  Console   Terminal ×   Jobs ×                                         ▬□
  ℝ  R 4.1.2 · ~/
  >
  > table(chickwts$feed)/nrow(chickwts)

     casein horsebean   linseed  meatmeal    soybean
  0.1690141 0.1408451 0.1690141 0.1549296 0.1971831
  sunflower
  0.1690141
  >
```

Naturally, you don't have to use a table for anything related to counts. We can also use a simple total of a suitable logical flag-vector—recall that in any mathematical approach of logical structures in R, 1 is automatically assigned to TRUEs and 0 I assigned to FALSEs.This will give you the sum of essential frequency, but you'll need to do division by the overall sample size to get a proportion. Furthermore, determining the mean of a logical flag vector is the same as doing this. To calculate the quantity of chickens fed soybean, for example, observe the given an example where we did two computations to provide the same answer of 0.197:

```
1  table(chickwts$feed=="soybean")/nrow(chickwts)
2  |
3
```

2:1   (Top Level) ÷   R :

Console   Terminal   Jobs

R R 4.1.2 · ~/
> table(chickwts$feed=="soybean")/nrow(chickwts)

     FALSE   TRUE
0.8028169 0.1971831
>

Variance

The previous central metrics give you a decent idea of where your numerical measures are massed none the less the "mean," "median," and "mode" don't tell you how distributed your data are. Spread measurements are required for this. In addition to your eight hypothetical observations, xcal, which you have provided, we'll also create the following eight observations named ycal.

```
Xcal <- c(2,1.3,2.7,2,3,2,2.2,4.8)
Ycal <- c(3,2,5,3,2,1.2,3.8)
```

Both data collections are different from each other, but they share the same mean, which is 2.5.

The "sample variance" is a measure of how much numeric observations differ from their "arithmetic mean." When we contrast variance to mean, it becomes a specific demonstration of the

74

average squared distance of numerical data. The sample variance s2x for a collection of "n" numeric dimensions categorized "x = x1, x2,..., xn" is provided by the subsequent, where "x" is a "sample mean" specified in the calculation. Following the variance formula, " $s\,2\,x\;=\;(x1\,-\,\overline{mean})2\,+\,(x2\,-\,mean)2\,+\,...+(xn\,-\,\overline{mean})2/n\,-\,1$." If we put those 8 observations of Xcal into this formula. We get the answer of 1.122, respectively.

Standard deviation

The root of variance becomes the standard deviation when calculated. This offers a value easy - to - interpret with regard to the scale of the initial observations. As the "variance" is a demonstration of the "average squared distance." The "sample standard deviation" denoted by "s" is calculated by calculating the "square-root" of the equation for a sample of "n" numbers using the same notation." $s_x\;=\;\sqrt{x^2}\;=\;\sqrt{\frac{1}{n-1}\sum_{i=1}^{n}(x_i-\bar{x})^2}$"

The "standard deviation" of the following 8 imaginary numbers, for example, is as follows (to 3 decimals), depending on the sample variance obtained before 1.059.

To put it another way, 1.059 is the average distance between each observation and the mean.

Inter quartile range

The "interquartile range" is not calculated with regard to the "sample mean," unlike the sd, such as "standard deviation" and variance. The "interquartile range" calculates the measurement of the mid of "50%" of the given data or the "range of values" which falls inside a "25% quartile" on the sideways of the "median." As a result, the interquartile range is calculated as the change between our data's "upper" and" "lower" quartiles. Informally, "Qx (.)" denotes the "quantile function."

"var" for "variance," "sd" for "standard deviation," and "IQR" for" interquartile range" are direct "R" functions for determining these spread measurement

```
Untitled5    kjklj.R    Untitled6*    Untitled3*    Source
       Source on Save                                Source
1   xcal <- c(2,1.3,2.7,2,3,2,2.2,4.8)
2
3   Ycal <- c(3,2,5,3,2,1.2,3.8)
4
5
6   var(xcal)
7   sd(xcal)
8   IQR(xcal)
9   |

9:1     (Top Level)                                  R Script

Console   Terminal   Jobs
R  R 4.1.2 · ~/
> xcal <- c(2,1.3,2.7,2,3,2,2.2,4.8)
>
> Ycal <- c(3,2,5,3,2,1.2,3.8)
>
>
> var(xcal)
[1] 1.122857
> sd(xcal)
[1] 1.05965
> IQR(xcal)
[1] 0.775
>
```

Do the same thing with the ycal observations that have the same arithmetic mean as the xcal observations. The results of the computations are as follows:

```
      Untitled5    kjkij.R    Untitled6*    Untitled3*    »
            Source on Save                       Source
 1   Xcal <- c(2,1.3,2.7,2,3,2,2.2,4.8)
 2
 3   Ycal <- c(3,2,5,3,2,1.2,3.8)
 4
 5
 6   var(ycal)
 7   sd(ycal)
 8   IQR(ycal)
 9

 9:1     (Top Level)                              R Script

 Console   Terminal    Jobs

 R  R 4.1.2 · ~/
 > Xcal <- c(2,1.3,2.7,2,3,2,2.2,4.8)
 >
 > Ycal <- c(3,2,5,3,2,1.2,3.8)
 >
 >
 > var(ycal)
 [1] 1.622857
 > sd(ycal)
 [1] 1.273914
 > IQR(ycal)
 [1] 1.4
 >
```

Note:

The variance (and hence the standard deviation) has been defined
only in terms of the "sample estimator," which is operated
automatically in "R" and utilizes the divisor of "n—1" in the
procedure. When observations at hand reflect a sample of a wider
population, this is the formula to utilize. In these circumstances,
using the divisor n 1 provides a more accurate approximation of the
underlying population value, known as an unbiased estimate. As a
result, you are not really computing the "average squared distance,"

but maybe it is conceived in that way and will simply approach it as the sample size "n" grows.

Correlation & Covariance

It's typically important to analyze the connection among 2 numeric objects while examining data to detect "trends." For instance, we may anticipate a significant positive link between height and weight measurements—taller persons tend to weigh more. Handspan and hair length, on the other hand, could seem to have less of a connection. The concept of correlation, which requires covariance, is one of the most typical and simplest methods such relationships are measured and linked.

The "covariance" measures the change in variables that in what limit two numeric objects "change together," as well as the nature of that linking, no matter if it is positive or negative. For example, we possess a sample of numerical for n persons for two variables labeled "x = x1, x2,..., xn" and "y = y1, y2,..., yn," where "xi" corresponds to "Yi" for "I = 1,...,n." The "sample covariance" "Rx y" is calculated as follows, with "x" and "y" demonstrating the "sample means" of two sets of numerical:

$$\text{"rx y } = 1/ n - 1 \text{ where } \sum_{i-1}^{n}(xi - \bar{x})(yi - \bar{y})\text{"}$$

When you obtain a positive Rx y outcome, it means that a "positive linear relationship" is formed as x grows, and so does y. While you receive a "negative" result, it means there's a "negative linear connection" between two vectors x y, respectively. When Rx y = o, it means that the values of x and y do not have a linear relationship.

It does not matter in what order the variables appear in the formula, or we can simply say, "rx y ≡ ry x."

Now we look at the initial 8 demonstrative observations, which we'll refer to as Xcal - (2,1.3,2.7,2,3,2,2.2,4.8), and then another set of 8 observations, which I'll refer to as Ycal - (3,2,5,3,2,1.2,2.8,1). Notice that I added one more observation in y-cal. The reason for this addition is that we want to make sure both data sets have equal no. of observations. Otherwise, you will get an error "incompatible dimensions" we run the code.

Keep in mind that the "sample means" for both x,y is 2.5. These two sets of observations have the following sample covariance (rounded to three decimal places)

$$-0.363$$

Because the figure is a negative number, it implies that the observations in xcal and ycal point to a negative association.

Correlation helps you to dig further into the covariance by determining the intensity and direction of any relationship. Diverse forms of "correlation coefficients" are there none the less the utmost shared is "Pearson's product-moment correlation coefficient," which is R's default (and the estimate we'll use in this section). The "Pearson's sample correlation coefficient" x y is calculated by multiplying the "sample covariance" by the product of each data set's standard deviation. Formally, rx y corresponds to the covariance equation and sx and sy to the ordinary deviation equation.

$$\rho x\,y\ =\ rx\,y\,/sx\,sy$$

Which guarantees that "-1≤ p x y ≤ 1.

A complete negative linear connection arises when px y = -1. Any result <0 indicates a "negative association," and the connection weakens as the coefficient approaches 0 until px y = 0, indicating no relationship at all. A positive association emerges when the coefficient rises above 0 until px y = 1, which is considered to be a "perfect positive linear relationship."

But when we add the "standard deviations" for xcal and ycal (sx = 1.059 and sy = 1.274) together, we get the following.

$$\frac{-0.363}{1.059 \times 1.274} = -0.269$$

x y, like rx y, is positive; the result of -0.269 suggests a moderate-to-strong negative relationship between x and y observations. pxy ≡ py x

The "R" functions "cov" and "cor" are used to calculate model "covariance" and "correlation" all we are required are the 2 data vector for the calculations.

```
 1  xcal <- c (2,1.3,2.7,2,3,2,2.2,4.8)
 2  ycal <- c(3,2,5,3,2,1.2,2.8,1 )
 3  cov(xcal, ycal)
 4  cor(xcal,ycal)
 5  |
```

```
> cov(xcal, ycal)
[1] -0.3628571
> cor(xcal,ycal)
[1] -0.269754
```

These "binomial data" may be plotted as a group-up display.

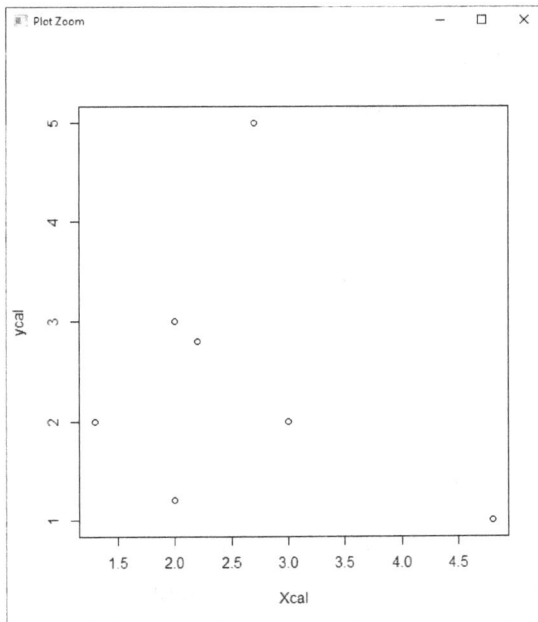

81

As previously stated, the "correlation coefficient" evaluates the identity of the "linear relationship" among "2 sets: of data objects. For example, if we observe the design made by the spots in the above picture and visualize making a perfectly "straight line" that characterizes all of them in the best manner, we can regulate the "strength of the linear association" of points by determining means of their closeness with each other to our line.

The value of x y will be closer to 1 or 1 for points closer to a "perfect straight line." Here the slope of the lines determines the direction—a "rising trend" a positive correlation is seen with the "line sloping upward toward the right." A "Lowering trend" where a negative correlation with the line sloping downward toward the right. In light of this, the projected "correlation coefficient" for the data presented earlier seems to be reasonable based on the preceding computations. In terms of the values in xcal and ycal, the points seem to rise in a roughly straight line, although this linear relationship is far from ideal.

It's crucial to keep in mind that correlation does not indicate causality. When you see a strong correlation between two variables, it doesn't always indicate that one causes the other. Even in the best-controlled conditions, proving causation is challenging.

Correlation is only a tool for determining the strength of a link.

As previously indicated, there are various ways to describe correlation "rank coefficients," to the same degree "Spearman's" and "Kendall's" "correlation coefficients," which vary from

"Pearson's estimate" in that they do not need a linear connection. These may also be accessed using the cor function's "optional method parameter." "Pearson's correlation coefficient," on the other hand, is the most often used and is linked to linear regression techniques.

Outliers

An outlier is a data point that doesn't seem to "fit" with the rest of the data. When compared to the rest of the data, it is clearly out of the ordinary or an abnormality. You could believe that such risky data did not originate with the same process that produced the additional data in certain circumstances, but there is no hard and fast numerical criterion for what defines an outlier.

I'll use two more vectors, "x" and "y," to provide a bivariate example:

```
X<- c(0.2,0.4,1.2,0.5,0.3,-1.8,0.7,0.8,-
0.9,-1.2)
Y<- c(-0.4,0.8,1.8,4.3,1.1,-3.1,-0.5,4.3,-
2.5,-110.0)
```

Now using the following code, I will execute the data set "x" and "y."

Source on Save

```
1
2   X<- c(0.2,0.4,1.2,0.5,0.3,-1.8,0.7,0.8,-0.9,-1.2)
3   Y<- c(-0.4,0.8,1.8,4.3,1.1,-3.1,-0.5,4.3,-2.5,-110.0)
4   plot(X,Y,axes =T, cex = 2,cex.axes= 1.5, cex.axes=1.5)
5   arrows(-0.5,-80,-0.94,-97,lwd=2)
6   text(-0.45,-74,labels="outlier?",cex=3)
```

6:40   (Top Level) ÷

Console   Terminal ×   Jobs ×

R 4.1.2 · ~/

```
> X<- c(0.2,0.4,1.2,0.5,0.3,-1.8,0.7,0.8,-0.9,-1.2)
> Y<- c(-0.4,0.8,1.8,4.3,1.1,-3.1,-0.5,4.3,-2.5,-110.0)
> plot(X,Y,axes =T, cex = 2,cex.axes= 1.5, cex.axes=1.5)
There were 12 warnings (use warnings() to see them)
> arrows(-0.5,-80,-0.94,-97,lwd=2)
> text(-0.45,-74,labels="outlier?",cex=3)
> |
```

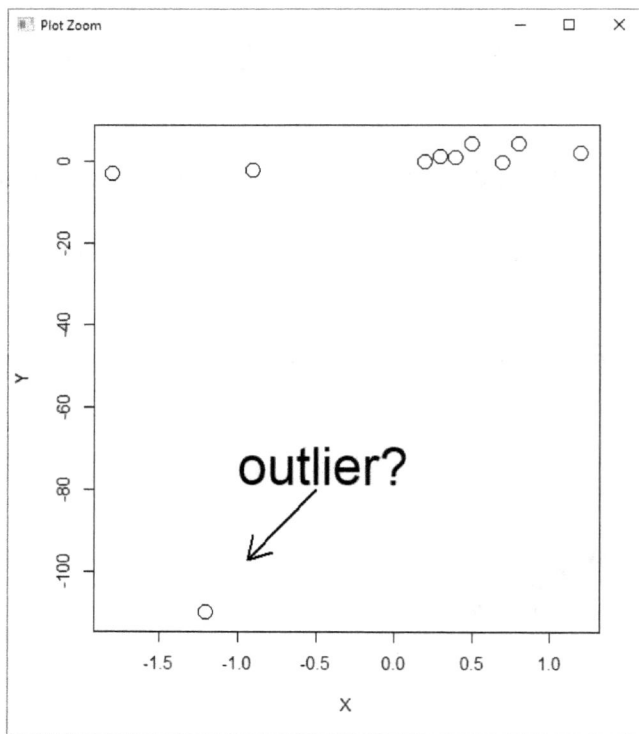

Outliers must be identified since they may have a significant influence on statistical computations and model fitting. As a consequence, many researchers may do an "exploratory" examination of the "data" by means of simple "summary statistics and data visualization" utensils before calculating findings in order to discover any outliers.

Outliers may arise naturally when the "outlier" is a "genuine" observation from the "population" when something may "polluted" that specific influence on the "sample," such as faulty "data entry." As per result, it is typical to eliminate any outliers arising from non-natural sources prior to analysis, although this isn't always straightforward since determining the reason for an outlier might be challenging. In certain circumstances, researchers offer their findings both ways, including and omitting any ostensible outliers.

Moreover, the impact of risky annotations on our "data analysis" is determined not just by their extremeness but rather by the statistics we aim to produce. The "sample mean," for instance, is very subtle to "outliers" and would fluctuate significantly while adding or eliminating them. Therefore, any figure that is dependent on the "mean," such as var or cov, would be impacted as well. Outliers have little effect on quantiles and associated statistics like the median or IQR. This trait is known as robustness in statistical terms.

Distributions of Sampling

The distribution of sampling is similar to any other "probability distribution" except that they are linked to a "random variable" called a "sample statistic."

Let us expect that the characteristics of the relevant sample distribution were known to us. (The "mean" and "standard deviation" of a "normal distribution," for example, or the rate of accomplishment in a "binomial distribution") none the less, in actuality, these variables are frequently unidentified. In such situations, we'd usually evaluate the amounts using a "sample."

Such statistic derived within a sample may be thought of as a "random variable," with the predictable rate serving as the realization of that "random variable." As a result, it is completely feasible that various samples from one population may offer dissimilar results for the existing statistic. "random variable" realizations are inherently changeable. Many statistical studies need the capacity to comprehend and simulate natural variation inherent in probable "sample statistics."

The center "balancing" point of a sampling distribution, like any other "probability distribution," is its "mean" The standard deviation, on the other hand, is denoted as a "standard error." The little alteration in terminology imitates the element that the "probabilities of interest" are now calculated from a sample of such data rather than being related to raw dimensions or observations per standard error. As a result, the theoretical formulae for different sampling distributions are based on

> (1) The initial "probability distributions" that are considered to have created the raw observation, and

> (2) The sample size.

We'll concentrate on 2 basic but readily recognized "statistics," a "single sample mean," and a "single sample percentage," and we'll explain the fundamental principles and present some examples in this part.

Distribution of "sample mean"

When summarising a data collection, the arithmetic mean is likely the most frequent metric of importance. The inherent variability in an expected "sample mean" is mathematically expressed.

'X' is the formal name for the random variable of interest. The mean of 'n' observations from a sample of random variable "X," as in "x1, x2,..., xn," is represented like this. The genuine "limited mean" "X" and true finite "standard deviation" such as "Ö X" are assumed for those observations. Depending on anyways you know the "standard deviation," the requirements for determining the probability distribution of a sample mean change.

Situation 1: Known Standard Deviation

The following are true if the real value of the "standard deviation X" is identified:

- "If "X" is normal, then the sampling distribution of X is also normal, with a mean of X and a "standard error" of X/n"

- "Even if "X" is not normal, the "sampling distribution" of 'X' is about normal, with 'mean μX' and "standard error" "$\sigma X/ \sqrt{n}$", and this approximation increases randomly as "n" increases. The "central limit theorem" is what it's usually called."

Situation 2: Unknown Standard Deviation

In fact, you're unlikely to distinguish the "actual standard deviation" of the "raw measurement distribution" from which you derived our sample data.

In such a case, it's common to exchange X with SX, which will be equivalent to the sampled data's standard deviation. However, this replacement provides more unpredictability, which has an impact on the sample mean "random variable's distribution."

- The sampling distribution of X's standardized values follows a "t-distribution" with "v = n-1 degrees of freedom" standardization is done using the SE sX/n .

- If "n" is also small, the rationality of this "t-based sampling distribution" of "X" must be dependent on the assumption that the "distribution of X is normal."

If the true "standard deviation" of the data and also the size of sample "n" are known, it determines the type of the sampling distribution of X. Normality happens even though the distribution of raw observations is indeed not regular, according to the CLT, however, this calculation is not accurately trustworthy if "n" is "small." It is a typical general law to use the "CLT" individually when "n" is less than 30. The sampling distribution is the t-distribution if sX, the "sample standard deviation" is used to derive the "standard error" of "X." (following standardization). Only if n is less than 30 is this considered credible.

For example

Assume that the daily maximum temperature in Johannesburg, South Africa, for the month of January, "With a mean of 24 degrees Celsius and a standard deviation of 1.6" per cent, trails a "normal distribution." As mentioned earlier, with a mean of 24 and a standard error of 1.6/ 5 0.716, the "sample distribution" of "X" will be normal; the "sampling distribution" of X for a sample of "size n = 5" will be normal, with a mean of 24 and a "standard error of 1.6/ 5 0.716". This may be done using the code from the previous section.

The sample distribution of X, in this case, is obviously a taller, skinnier "normal distribution" than the one associated with the data. This is reasonable. since an average of multiple measurements has less variability than raw, individual readings. Furthermore, if you increase the sample size, the inclusion of "n" in the "denominator" of the SE demands an extra accurate distribution around the "mean." This is reasonable once again because means will "vary less" among bigger sample data.

You may now pose numerous probability questions; keep in mind that the difference between the measurement and sampling distributions is critical. The following code, for example, calculates "Pr(X 23.5)", the probability of a high temperature of fewer than 23.5 degrees on a random day in January.

```
1    pnorm(23.5,mean=24,sd=1.6)
2
```

```
> pnorm(23.5,mean=24,sd=1.6)
[1] 0.3773303
>
```

{"The above line of code determines the chance that the sample mean will be less than 23.5 degrees, based on a sample of five random days in January (X 23.5)"}

```
1  pnorm(23.5,mean=24,sd=1.6/sqrt(5))
2  |
3
```

```
2:1    (Top Level) ÷

Console   Terminal   Jobs

R  R 4.1.2 · ~/
>
> pnorm(23.5,mean=24,sd=1.6/sqrt(5))
[1] 0.2423475
>
```

Other Statistics Sampling Distributions

We've only observed "sampling distributions" in terms of a single "sample mean" or "sample percentage" up to now., but many issues need more elaborate metrics. Nonetheless, the concepts discussed in this section may be applied to any statistic derived from a small sample size. Remember always that it is crucial to understand the variability related to your point estimation.

Under certain instances, such as the ones discussed up until now, the "sampling distribution" is "parametric" This implies that the "probability distribution's" operational (math) structure is defined and is solely reliant on the inputs of the defined model parameters. As you can see from this chapter's usage of the "normal distribution," this is sometimes conditional on the fulfillment of particular criteria. You may not know the shape of the relevant sample distribution for other statistics; in this instance, you may utilize computer simulation to derive the requisite probabilities.

You'll continue to look at statistics related to "parametric sampling" distributions aimed at popular models and tests throughout the rest of the journey in this chapter and the next chapters.

Moreover, only one side of the coin is the variability of an expected amount. The problem of statistical bias is also crucial. Whereas "natural variability" is linked to "random error bias" is linked to "systematic error" This indicates that when the sample size rises, a biassed statistic does not settle down on the "factual parameter value." Bias may be caused by flaws in a "data collection" as well as a poor estimation of the statistical interest. "Bias" is an unpleasant feature of almost any predictor and/or quantitative evaluation unless it can be evaluated and eliminated, and that is often challenging, if not impossible, in practice. As a consequence, we've solely worked with "unbiased statistical estimators" thus far (countless of them we are already acquainted with, such as the "arithmetic mean"), and we'll keep doing so in the long term.

An Average Interval

The "sampling distribution" of a "single sample mean" is mostly determined by whether we know the correct "standard deviation" of the fresh data, X, as you learned earlier. The "CLT" then provides a "symmetric sampling distribution" This would be typical if we learn the actual values of "X" and "t" based upon "v = n 1 df" if we have to calculate X using the "sample standard deviation" s— assuming the size of the sample for this "sample mean: is about" n 3o". (This is common in practice). The "standard error" is estimated by dividing the "standard deviation" by taking out the "square root" of "n."

Because the CLT does not apply when n is small, we may additionally adopt that the "raw observations" are regularly spread.

To create an acceptable interval, we should first determine the crucial value. The CI is symmetric by definition; therefore, this interprets as a "central probability" of one (1). In the lower tail, it's around the mean, and in the upper tail, it's the same.

We are returning to Johannesburg, South Africa's mean daily maximum temperatures in January, as described in the previous section. Assume you know the data are normally distributed but not the real mean X (which is 24) or the "true standard deviation X" (that is estimated at 1.6). Let's say we've made the subsequent set of 5 "independent observations" in the same manner you did earlier:

Untitled1* ×   Untitled7* ×   Untitled1* ×   Untitled2* ×

```
  Source on Save   Q  ⁄  ▾                    → Run
1   x.sample<- rnorm(n=5, mean = 24, sd= 1.6)
2
3   x.sample
4   |
```

4:1   (Top Level) ⟂

Console   **Terminal** ×   **Jobs** ×

```
R  R 4.1.2 · ~/
> x.sample<- rnorm(n=5, mean = 24, sd= 1.6)
>
> x.sample
[1] 21.52684 24.54566 24.85552 22.50822 25.55093
>
```

Because we're concerned with the "sample mean" and its "sampling distribution," we'll need to compute the "sample mean x," the "sample standard deviation s," and the "corresponding standard error" of the "sample mean, s/ n."

```
1    x.mean <- mean(x.sample)
2    x.mean
3    x.sd <- sd(x.sample)
4    x.sd
5    x.se<- x.sd/sqrt(5)
6    x.se|
```

6:5   (Top Level) ⬍

Console   **Terminal** ×   **Jobs** ×

R 4.1.2 · ~/
```
> x.mean <- mean(x.sample)
> x.mean
[1] 23.79743
> x.sd <- sd(x.sample)
> x.sd
[1] 1.700865
> x.se<- x.sd/sqrt(5)
> x.se
[1] 0.76065
>
```

Let us pretend the goal is to create a "95% confidence interval" for the genuine, "unknown mean X." For the appropriate sample distribution, this means 0.05 (the entire amount of tail probability). Given that the raw data are "normal" and that we're consuming "s" (rather than "X"), the "t-distribution" with "n-1 = 4 degrees of freedom" is the suitable distribution. This must be in either tail for a "central area of 0.95 under this curve". The (positive) critical value is determined by using "R's q functions" with a complete "lower tail area." We can achieve this by giving the relevant function a probability of 1 /2 = 0.975.

```
1  1-0.05/2
2  critical <- qt(0.975,df=4)
3  critical
```

3:9   (Top Level)

Console | Terminal | Jobs

R R 4.1.2 · ~/
> 1-0.05/2
[1] 0.975
> critical <- qt(0.975,df=4)
> critical
[1] 2.776445
>

Various Intervals

The importance of relating an estimator (or sample statistic) to the idea of variation is shown by the two basic instances mentioned previously. Of course, "confidence intervals" could be built for any number, and in my upcoming book, I'll show you how to examine variations between 2 means and 2 proportions using "confidence intervals," as well as "ratios of categorical counts." The conventional error equations for these more complicated statistics are different. But the accompanying "sampling distributions," there is an asymmetry that can be seen present through the "normal curves" and "t-curves" (provided certain normal expectations are fulfilled); therefore equation still applies.

A confidence interval attempts to demarcate a center region of 1 from the "sample distribution of interest" with asymmetric "sampling distributions." In such instances, though, a "symmetric CI" that is based on a particular, standardized critical rate as shown in the calculation makes little sense. Similarly, you could not know the sample distribution's functional, parametric shape and so be unwilling to make any distributary expectations, like "symmetry" In such circumstances, an alternate route grounded on the "raw quantiles" (or approximated "raw quantiles") of the ostensibly "asymmetric sampling distribution" might be followed. Consuming specified "quantile values" to demarcate indistinguishable /2 upper- and lower-tail sections is an acceptable way of constructing a usable interval that reflects possible real parameter values while being delicate to the structure of that "sampling distribution" of "interest."

Final comments

The conventional remark regarding the understanding of any "CI" refers to a "degree of confidence" in where the "real parameter value" resides, but an extra technically valid interpretation should take into account and explain the construction's probabilistic character. The more accurate interpretation, given a "100(1) per cent" level of confidence, is as follows:

We'll assume that the exact "corresponding parameter value" collapses inside the boundaries of "100(1) per cent" of those arrays over many examples of similar scope and from the same "population," where Class Intervals of similar confidence level is built with detail to the identical measurement from individually sampled individuals.

This is due to the fact that the sampling distribution theory represents the variability in several samples, not just the one that was collected. It must be problematic to see the difference between these and the often used "confidence statement" at first look, but this is critical to understand the technically accurate meaning, especially when a CI is generally determined based on just one sample.

Chapter 6

Control Structure

Control structures are programming constructs that allow you to have more control over a program's execution. A script would normally run line by line in a top-to-bottom (or top-down) manner. Control structures can be used to change the execution flow. As control structures, R provides decision-making components and loops for this purpose.

Lists

The list is a very practical data structure that is used to combine any number of R objects and structures together. A logical array, A numeric matrix, a factor object, and a single character string might all be included in a single list.

A list can even be used as a piece of another list. We'll learn how to access, construct, and edit components of these stretchy structures in this section.

Making a list is similar to making a vector. You provide the list function of the components you want to include, separated by commas.

List creation

The function *list()* is used to generate a list in r Studio. For example, you can create a list by using a random variable. Let's say you want to add details of your dear friend jhon so, in r studio; you will create a random_list (variable), then following the = sign, you will use the list() function and add details using the following script on r studio

```
jhon = list("john," 27, 7.3, "Muslim")
```

And see, you just created a list. Now you can add random numbers or any data that you want to be enlisted.

```
Console   Terminal    Jobs
R   R 4.1.2 · ~/
> jhon = list("john", 27, 7.3, "muslim")
> jhon
[[1]]
[1] "john"

[[2]]
[1] 27

[[3]]
[1] 7.3

[[4]]
[1] "muslim"

> |
```

List elements

Suppose you have a list, and you only need a specific part of that list in your code. You can call its elements separately by list name(element number) and hit enter. For example, I want to add jhon's religion to my list, so I will type

John[[4]] and hit enter, and I will get the word Muslim on my screen.

The component names are always given when using the names function.

Returned as double-quoted character strings. If you're stating names, though.

At the time a list is constructed (within the list command) or when extracting members via names, the names move in without quotations (or, let's say, they are not surrounded by quotes) when using the dollar operator.

Logical operation on the list

Using is.list = (list name) function also allows you to find whether a particular variable is a list or not, for example. If I type is.list= (jhon) in r studio, it will return as true, so you can use this function for configuration purposes

Merging two or more lists

As you know, you can create as many lists as you want. There is one more feature that I want to talk about, and that is merging lists together. Previously I created a list named jhon. Let's say I have another list named Nida, and I want to merge these lists, so I will simply create a new variable named X and assign both lists to the new variable

x <- c(jhon, Nida). After that, I will just print X, and both lists will be merged. See the following picture for an example.

```
Console   Terminal   Jobs
R  R 4.1.2 · ~/
[[1]]
[1] "nida"

[[2]]
[1] 23

[[3]]
[1] 6.1

[[4]]
[1] "muslim"

> x <- c(jhon, nida)
> x
[[1]]
[1] "john"

[[2]]
[1] 27

[[3]]
[1] 7.3

[[4]]
[1] "muslim"

[[5]]
[1] "nida"
```

Decision making

Decision-making statements in R enable you to determine whether or not to execute a piece of code based on a condition. In every programming language, making decisions is critical. Conditional statements are also known as Decision-Making statements.

We'll need to manage the order and flow of performance of our code to develop increasingly complex R applications. Making the execution of some lines of code conditional is one of the most basic ways to achieve this.

The loop that recaps a code block a specified number of times is another basic control technique. We'll use the if statement and-else

102

statement for loop and while loop and further control structures to examine these essential programming principles in this chapter.

IF statement

We use the if statement to find whether a statement is true or not. The if statement is essential for determining which actions are performed in a specified section of code. The "if" A statement is used to run a piece of code. If a condition is met, it is said to be true. Depending on whether a condition turns out to be TRUE or FALSE, following structures allows a computer to behave otherwise. For example, if you look at the following picture. Here we also get Boolean expressions that evaluate true and false, respectively.

```
      Source on Save    Q                    Run    Source
1  x <-5
2  if(x< 7)
3
4  {print("true")} |
```

```
4:17   (Top Level)                                          R Script

Console   Terminal   Jobs
R  R 4.1.2 · ~/
> x <-5
> if(x< 7)
+
+ {print("true")}
[1] "true"
>
```

After the if keyword, the condition is enclosed in parentheses. This condition must be a logical expression with only one logical value (TRUE or FALSE).

The code in the brackets{} will be run if it is TRUE. The code in the brackets is skipped if the condition isn't met. After the closing brace, R continues to execute any code. (or does nothing). For example, see the following explanation.

First, I assign value 5 to variable x. then I use the if function to check if 5 is less than 7, and then using curly braces, I command it if the statement is true, print true. And here is the result. Try it in your r studio for practice. So since 5 is less than 7 it turned out to be a TRUE value. The rules apply here too. We use characters in quotation marks. Remember each detail discussed previously to achieve perfection.

Note: Each line following the first is preceded by a + when you submit the if statement to the console. These + marks don't signify any type of mathematical addition, and in fact, they indicate that R is waiting for further commands before starting to execute. When a { is opened, for example, R will not do anything until the section is closed with a r }. We won't display this repeated code transmitted to the console from the editor in future instances to prevent redundancy.

ELSE statement

The IF expression can be followed by an option which is else expression. So in the previous expression, you only get one option if you change the values. The statement will simply not print anything if the statement is wrong or false. You can use an "else statement" If the condition comes out to be FALSE, you may have something else happen. Here's a pseudocode example: So here we use the else statement.

```
helloworld.r*
      Source on Save                    Run          Source
 1  x <-5
 2  if(x< 4)
 3
 4  {print("true")}  else{print("false")}|


                                                      R Script
 4:38    (Top Level)

Console  Terminal  Jobs
R   R 4.1.2 · ~/
>  x <-5
>  if(x< 7)
+
+  {print("true")}
[1] "true"
>  x <-5
>  if(x< 4)
+
+  {print("true")}  else{print("false")}
[1] "false"
>
```

In the above picture, you can see I added the else expression right where the "IF" statement was ending. Remember, if you do not start the other expression right after the IF expression, you will get an error.

So I changed values and made the statement false, and hereafter executing the else expression, I got the result as false. You set the

105

condition, then put the code to run if the condition turns out to be TRUE in the first set of brackets. Then you state the "else" tailed by another set of brackets in which we may put code that will run if the condition is "FALSE."

Keep practicing. Only practice can make you an expert in this language.

ELSE-IF statement

There can only be one other statement in an if statement. This implies that if you don't use nested if-else statements, you can only check for one condition. Another feature of the if-else construct is that it allows you to test for several conditions. The else-if construct is what it's called. The else-if code block cannot be used on its own; it must be included in the if-else construct. This is how it works: there will be an optional else statement, a necessary if statement with a given expression, and several else-if statements with their own expressions. The if statement's expression will be tested first, and if it calculates to TRUE, the if block will be performed, with the remainder of the blocks being disregarded. The expression of the immediate (next) else-if block will be tested if the expression evaluates to FALSE. If it calculates to TRUE, the block in question will be performed, while the rest of the blocks will be ignored. If that expression also evaluates to FALSE, the following else if block (if present) will be searched, and so on until a TRUE expression is discovered. The else block (if present) will be invoked if none of the expressions evaluates to TRUE.

In the above picture, I created a scenario of a match. The current score is 120. If the score is 121, we win the match. On the other hand, if the score is 120, it will be a tie. And in the other expression, I simply mean that if the score is more than 120, "we lost" the match. So as you can see, the program ignored the first option and followed the second option here.

Switch expression

The switch is a decision-making mechanism found in many simple "programming languages" such as "C/C++," "Python," and "Java" that aids in making a decision when an expression can have numerous outputs. This eliminates the need to write many if, otherwise, if, and else statements, maybe nested ones. The switch is a function provided in R that returns a value. This method works in a similar way to switching constructs in other programming languages, although it does so in a slightly different way. A switch is an R function that checks an expression against a list of elements.

```
1  y <-"120"
2  x<-switch(
3    y,
4    "119" = "we lost",
5    "120" = "its a tie",
6    "121" = "we won"
7  )
8  print (x)
```

```
R  R 4.1.2 · ~/
> y <-"120"
> x<-switch(
+   y,
+   "119"= "we lost",
+   "120"= "its a tie",
+   "121" = "we won"
+ )
> print (x)
[1] "its a tie"
>
```

The expression is first evaluated. Consider the case where the expression equals a number, let's say 120. This number is used to find the element's serial number and choose it. NULL is returned if the number is less than 0 or larger than the number of entries in the list (i.e., No element is returned). Consider the fact that the list contains three items. This is how the simplified syntax might look:

The element 1> will be returned if the equation evaluates to 1. If it evaluates to 2, it will return element 2; if it evaluates to 3, it will return element 3>. The value will be returned as NULL if it is evaluated to a number less than 1 or larger than 3 (total number of entries in the list).

LOOPS STATEMENT

Loops are another common programming constructs that are used to repeat a piece of code. While Loop, repeat loop, and for loop are the three loops available in R. The "for loop" rerun code element by element as it progresses along a vector, whereas "while loop" merely rerun code till a "specified condition" calculates to "FALSE." We'll take a look at each of these.

For Loop

When we need to perform a chunk of code for a particular quantity of iterations, the "For loop" is a more efficient loop to utilize.

To run this loop, you'll need a list or a vector. The number of items in the vector will be the same as the number of times this loop will run. Each iteration will grab an element from the vector and save it in the value> variable. The next element will be retrieved during the following iteration, and so on until the last element is obtained. The vector does not have to be atomic or contain just integers; elements of any data type will suffice. Here's a snippet of code that uses the for loop to display letters one through seven. The (:) operator will be used to fill a vector first, and the for loop will be used to display them one by one.

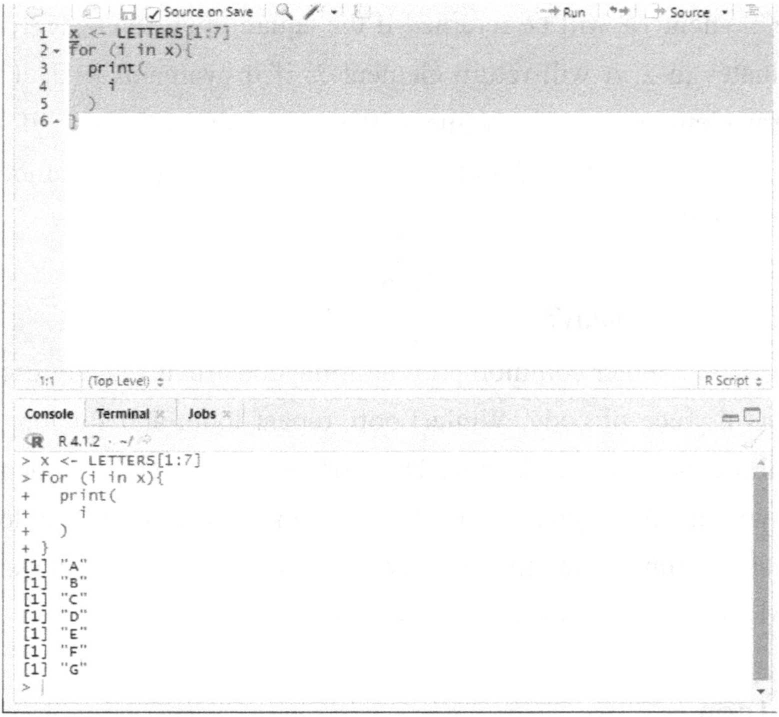

```
1  x <- LETTERS[1:7]
2 ▾ for (i in x){
3      print(
4        i
5      )
6 ▴ }
```

```
> x <- LETTERS[1:7]
> for (i in x){
+    print(
+      i
+    )
+ }
[1] "A"
[1] "B"
[1] "C"
[1] "D"
[1] "E"
[1] "F"
[1] "G"
>
```

In the above picture, you can see the loop repeated itself until it reached the seventh letter. Try all the 26 alphabets and see the for loop repeat for practice.

You need to generate some vectors to keep information about the list members before writing the "for loop." "is.mat" to show if the individual argument is a "matrix (with "Yes" / "No")" we use nr and nc to stock the quantity of columns and rows. And we use "data type" to represent the "data type" of every matrix.

Loop index or loop value

Consider that the distinction amid by using the loop index to denote items in a loop vector and using it to denote vector indexes. These two ways are used in the following two loops to print double each number in x:

```
RStudio

File   Edit   Code   View   Plots   Session   Build   Debug   Profile   Tools   Help

       Go to file/function            Addins

 Untitled1*      helloworld.r      Untitled2*      Untitled3*

      Source on Save        Run      Source

   1   x <- c(2,3,4,5)
   2-     for (i in x) {
   3          print(2*i)
   4-     }
   5
   6
   7- for (i in  1:length(x)) {
   8        print(2*x[i])
   9-   }
  10
  11

  10:1    (Top Level)                                              R Script

Console   Terminal     Jobs

 R   R 4.1.2 · ~/
 >      for (i in x) {
 +          print(2*i)
 +      }
 [1] 4
 [1] 6
 [1] 8
 [1] 10
 >
 >
 >
 > for (i in  1:length(x)) {
 +      print(2*x[i])
 +   }
 [1] 4
 [1] 6
 [1] 8
 [1] 10
 >
```

The first loop prints the value of each element multiplied by two, using the loop index I to directly show the items in "x." We use "*i*" to characterize numbers in order "*1:length (x)*" On the other hand, in the second loop These integers make up all of the *x's* available

111

index locations, which you use to extract "*x's* elements" (multiplying each ingredient by 2 once more and displaying the outcome). Using vector index places allows greater freedom in terms of how you may utilize the loopindex, despite the fact that it takes a little longer form. When your demands demand more sophisticated loops, like in the next example, this will become evident. Now, let's create a more complicated list of matrixes.

Let's say now we want to develop any code that inspects some list objects and gathers data about some matrix objects that are kept as list members.

Consider the list below:

```
"list_1 <-
list(simple_11=c(12,13.1),sample_2
=matrix(1:6,2,2),sample_3 =
matrix(c(T,T,F,T,F,F),3,2),sample_4 ="this
is string",sample_5= matrix(c( "red",
"yellow", "orange","green" )))print(list_1"
```

You've developed *"list_1"*, which is made up of three matrixes with different sizes and types of data. We'll construct a "for loop," which will verify whether any element of a list like the one in the above example is a "matrix."

Uncertainty turned out to be a matrix; the loop will obtain the matrix's no. of "rows and columns" as well as its data type.

We need to generate some vectors to keep information about the list members before writing the "for loop" " is.mat" to show if every associate is a "matrix (with "Yes" / "No")" to keep track of how many columns and rows there are nc and nr for each matrix is used, and" to represent the type of data of each matrix are all stored in name "data.type".

```
name <- names(list_1)
print(name)
is_mat <- rep(NA , length(list_1))
print(is_mat)
nrow <- is_mat
ncolumn <- is_mat
data_type <- is_mat
```

As a name, we save the titles of the *"list_1"* elements. We also set up nc, nr, data. Type, is.mat, all of these are allocated length(*"list_1"*) vectors filled with NAs. Your "for loop," which we're now prepared to construct, will update these values as needed. In the editor, type the following code:

113

| Untitled1* | Untitled7* | Untitled1* | Untitled2* | Untitled4* | Untitled5 | Untitled6* |

```
1
2  for (i in 1:length(list_1)) {
3      member <- list_1[[i]]
4      if (is.matrix(member)){
5
6          ncolumn[i] <- ncol(member
7                    nrow[i] <- nrow(member)
8                    is_mat[i] <- "yes")
9          data_type[i] <- class(as.vector(member))}else {
10         is_mat[i] <- "no"
11     }
12  }
13  bar <- data.frame(name, nrow, is_mat,ncolumn,data_type,stringsAsFactors = FALSE)
14  bar
15
```

We will start by Setting up the loop index "I" to increase over the index locations of *list 1* (1:length(*list 1*)) at first. The first instruction is to write the list in the braced code 1 observation at location i to the object observation. Then, using "is.matrix", you can see if that member is a matrix. If this is the case, do the following steps.

The ith element of nc and nr is agreed to the no. of "columns and rows" of the member, individually, and the " i^{th} " element of "datatype" is agreed to the outcome of the class. This closing command utilises the class function to discover the data type of the elements after coercing the matrix into a vector using as.vector.

If the condition fails because a member isn't a matrix, the relevant entrance in "is_mat" is agreed to "No," The characteristics in the subsequent vectors, on the other hand, remain unaltered; therefore, they are certain to remain NA.

Following the "loop," the vectors are used to form a data frame bar (notice the practice of "stringsAsFactors=FALSE" to avoid the character string vectors in a bar from being routinely transformed to factors; After running the code, the bar should appear like this:

```
Source

Console   Terminal   Jobs
R  R 4.1.2 · ~/
> print(bar)
          name is_mat nrow ncolumn data_type
1 simple_11   <NA>   NA    NA         NA
2  sample_2   <NA>   NA    NA         NA
3  sample_3   <NA>   NA    NA         NA
4  sample_4     no   NA    NA         NA
5  sample_5   <NA>   NA    NA         NA
>
```

As you notice, this corresponds to the type of the matrixes in list_1.

Nesting "for loop"

We can nest "loops" the same way you would layer the "if statements." While a "for loop" is embedded within an additional "for loop," the "inner loop" is completed before the "outer loop's" loop index is increased, at which time the "inner loop" is repeated. In your R terminal, create the following objects:

```
35
36
37   lv1<- 11:13
38   print(lv1)
39   lv2 <- 20:17
40   print(lv2)
41   list_2 <- matrix(NA ,length(lv1), length(lv2))
42   list_2
43
44
43:1    (Top Level) ‡

Console   Terminal   Jobs
R  R 4.1.2 · ~/
> list_2
       [,1] [,2] [,3] [,4] [,5]
[1,]   NA   NA   NA   NA   NA
[2,]   NA   NA   NA   NA   NA
[3,]   NA   NA   NA   NA   NA
>
```

115

The looping loop that follows multiplies each integer in lv1 (which is loopvector1) by each integer in lv2 to fill list_2. Now use the following script.

```
"for (i in 1: length(lv1)) {
   for (j in 1:length(lv2)) {
      list_2[i,j] <- lv1[i]*lv2[j]


   }


}
list_2"
```

```
43
44
45 ▾ for (i in 1: length(lv1)) {
46 ▾    for (j in 1:length(lv2)) {
47          list_2[i,j] <- lv1[i]*lv2[j]
48
49 ▴    }
50
51 ▴ }
52   list_2
53
54
55
56
57
```

54:1   (Top Level) ⇕

Console   Terminal ×   Jobs ×

R R 4.1.2 · ~/

```
>
>
> for (i in 1: length(lv1)) {
+    for (j in 1:length(lv2)) {
+       list_2[i,j] <- lv1[i]*lv2[j]
+
+    }
+
+ }
> list_2
       [,1] [,2] [,3]
[1,]   220  209  198
[2,]   240  228  216
[3,]   260  247  234
>
```

116

It's worth noting that each usage of for in a nested loop requires a different loopindex.

The loopindex in this situation defines that "I" is for the "outer loop" similarly "j" for the "inner loop".

While the block of code is running, the inner "loop" starts with I being allocated 1, and then j is assigned 1. The inner loop's single instruction is to allocate the creation of the "ith" element of lv1 and the "jth" element of lv2 to list 2's "row I" "column j." The "inner loop" is repeated until "j" exceeds distance (lv2) and seals the opening row of list 2. After that, I am incremented, and the inner loop is restarted. When "I" touches "length(lv1)" and the matrix is full, the operation is finished.

Inner "loop" vectors can be configured to equal the loop index of the outer "loop's" current value. Here's an example using lv1 and lv2 from before.

RStudio

File Edit Code View Plots Session Build Debug Profile Tools Help

```
44
45 - for (i in 1: length(lv1)) {
46 -   for (j in 1:length(lv2)) {
47       list_2[i,j] <- lv1[i]*lv2[j]
48
49 -   }
50
51 - }
52   list_2
53
54
55   list_2<- matrix(NA,length(lv1),length(lv2))
56
57   list_2
58 - for (i in 1:length(lv1)) {
59 -   for (j in 1:i) {
60   list_2[i,j] <- lv1[i]+lv2[j]
61 -   }
62
63 - }
64   list_2
65  |
66
67
68
69
70
71
72
```

```
"list_2<- matrix(NA,length(lv1),length(lv2))
list_2
for (i in 1:length(lv1)) {
  for (j in 1:i) {
list_2[i,j] <- lv1[i]+lv2[j]
  }

}
list_2"
```

118

```
RStudio
File  Edit  Code  View  Plots  Session  Build  Debug  Profile  Tools  Help

⊕  ▾  ◯  ⇄  ▾  🖫 🖫  🖳  ⇨ Go to file/function        ▾ Addins ▾

Source

Console    Terminal ×    Jobs ×

R  R 4.1.2 · ~/
> list_2
      [,1] [,2] [,3]
[1,]   31   NA   NA
[2,]   32   31   NA
[3,]   33   32   31
> for (i in 1:length(lv1)) {
+    for (j in 1:i) {
+ list_2[i,j] <- lv1[i]+lv2[j]
+    }
+
+ }
> list_2
      [,1] [,2] [,3]
[1,]   31   NA   NA
[2,]   32   31   NA
[3,]   33   32   31
>
```

The sum of lv1[i] and lv2[j] is filled into the ith row, jth column element of list_2. The inner loop values for j, on the other hand, are now determined by the worth of "I." while "i is 1", for example, the "inner loop" vector remains "1:1", which means the "inner loop" merely runs just the once before its return to the "outer loop." The inner loop vector is 1:2 when i is 2, and so on.

Each row of list_2 is only half-filled as a result of this. When writing loops in this manner, extra caution is required. The values for j, for example, are dependent on the length of lv1. Therefore if length(lv1) is bigger than length, an error will occur (lv2).

Nesting any number of for loops is possible, but if nested loops are utilized inefficiently, the computational cost might become an issue. Because loops increase computational complexity in general, you should constantly ask yourself, "Can I accomplish this in a vector-oriented fashion?" while writing R code. Only use an iterative, looping strategy if the individual actions aren't practicable or easy to accomplish in bulk.

While Loop

Where for loop is used to execute until the assigned numbers are not completely displayed. we should keep this in mind or should be capable of quickly determining the total of intervals the "loop" must be repeated in order to utilize it for loops. The while loop can be used in cases when you don't have knowledge of how many times the required activities need to perform. A "while loop" continues to run and keeps repeating itself while a given "condition" proves to be "TRUE," and it looks like this:

"While loop" only runs until it finds the matching condition. Here we also use Boolean conditions most of the time, such as TURE or FALSE.

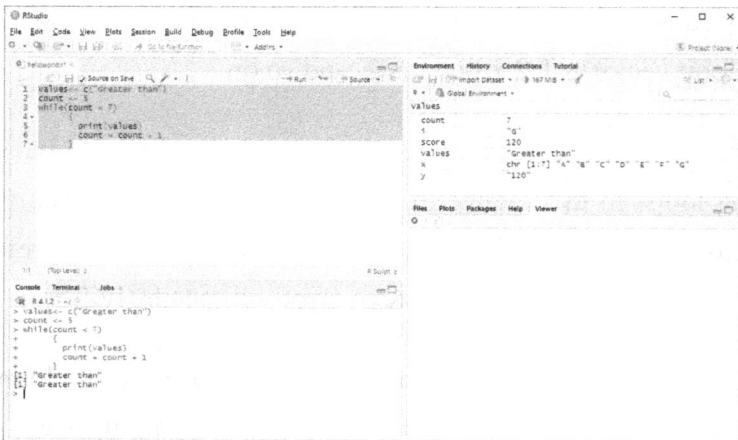

The number of times a while loop repeats is controlled by a single logical-valued loop condition. The loop condition is assessed when the loop is executed. Whether the "condition" turns out as "TRUE," the "code" in the brackets will perform line by line until it is finished, after which the "loop" condition is tested another time. The "loop" will end simply when the "condition" estimates as "FALSE," and it's instantly. The "code" in the bracket wills do not repeat one final time.

This indicates that the actions in the brackets should force the "loop" to depart in some way, by influencing the "loop" condition or by stating "break." That we will see later. If not, the "loop" will run indefinitely, causing the console to freeze (and, relying on the actions provided inside the brackets, R may crash (due to memory limits). When this happens, you stop the loop via the R user interface by hitting ESC or choosing the Stop button in the top menu. In other words, the supplied condition is tested when the while loop is encountered.

The statements inside the while block are performed one by one if it evaluates to TRUE. A loop iteration is a process in which a collection of statements is performed one by one, starting with the first statement and ending at the end of the block. The condition is checked again when the execution control reaches the end of the block, and if it calculates to TRUE, the block of code is performed again. This cycle will continue until the condition calculates to TRUE. The block of code will not run if it calculates to FALSE. The loop will continue to execute if the situation never calculates to FALSE; this is known as an endless loop.

Repeat Loop

The repeat loop does not include a termination condition. Therefore, it will continue to run indefinitely. The only way to stop this loop from running is to use the break statement. It's best to manually check for a condition inside the loop and then use the break statement to end it. Consider the following code piece, which uses a repeat loop to show a random sentence. When the value hits 7, we manually end it with a break statement.

Chapter 7

Functions, Strings and Factors

A function is a piece of code that performs single or multiple tasks. The sketch of an R function is as follows,

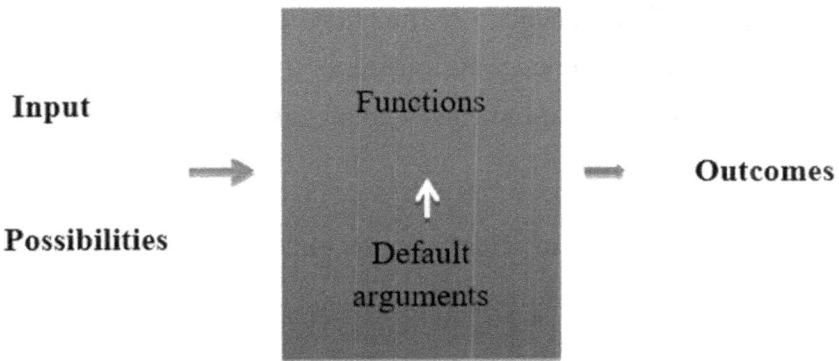

Methods, routines, and sub-routines are all terms used to describe functions. One of the main reasons for the existence of functions is to prevent rewriting the same code repeatedly. Hence, enhancing the reusability of code. We've already seen it print, cat, seq, and other built-in functions that Someone has previously written. The print function is a function that we may all use to display things on the screen. Consider what it would be like if we had to engage with code. Every time we intended to display a message, we used the device's output stream on the screen for a simple massage. Functions allow us to reuse the previous code with a little bit of changing. We'll learn how to write our own functions. First, we will discuss the term function in detail.

Definition:

There are four essential parts in the definition of the function.

1. Name: A function name is a name given to it in order to distinguish it from other functions. The same principles apply to naming a function as they do to naming a variable.

2. List of arguments: A function can optionally receive variables to conduct various tasks. Local variables are used to store these arguments. Parameters are another name for arguments.

3. Body of function: This is the section of a function where the actual work is carried out.

4. The body of a function is made up of statements. Return values: Optionally, a function can return a value to the caller function.

Creating a function:

Using the above definition, we can create our own function in RStudio. We start with assigning a name to the function in our case, let's say "x," then assign a function that is a keyword in RStudio. Using parenthesis "()," we declare our" **input**," which is the general argument. There could be multiple arguments. Then we add a set of curly braces "{}." To avoid error, we always hit "enter" after curly braces. The values we assign in the curly braces are considered a group setting that will execute all at once. Inside curly braces, we declare the **"output"** followed by <- signs. Here we need to command the function to do something such as addition, multiplication, etc, followed by curly braces again, and in this set of curly braces, we write our "input."

The last step is the return function which will declare the output of the entire function.

For example:

```
Function_name <- function(inputs){
Output_value<- do_something(input)
Return (output_value)
```

That's how you create a function in RStudio.

Arguments:

The arguments may be objects (information, formulae, phrases, and so on), with some of them being specified by default in the function. The user can change these "default values" by providing choices. An "R" function cannot need any parameters: All parameters are either defined by default (or their values may be altered using the options), or they are not declared at all. The function has no arguments declared. We'll go through how to utilise and construct functions in greater depth later.

Lazy evaluation is a key feature in many high-level programming languages when it comes to managing arguments. This usually denotes the notion that terms are only calculated when they are required. This also claims to the parameters in that they are only accessible and utilized when they occur in the function body.

Let's have a look at how R functions identify and use parameters while running. As a working example, we'll create a "function" that examines a comprehensive list of "matrix objects" and attempts to post multiply each with another matrix provided as a second argument. The result is saved and returned in a fresh list by the function. The function must produce a character "string" advising the operator of these facts if no matrixes are in the specified list or if no acceptable matrixes are present. If there are matrixes in the supplied list, you can assume they are numeric.

Calling a function

In the following example, we will implement this function to calculate something. Let's say the volume of a plant named Tulsi. I assume that we all know that volume can be calculated using the plant's length, height, and width.

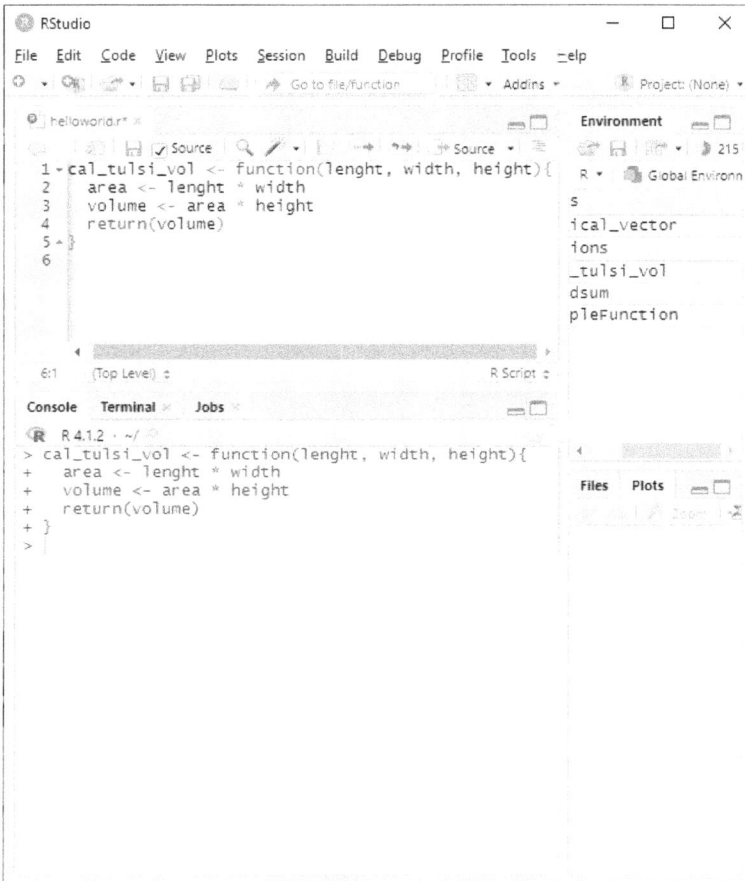

When a function is defined, it does not run on its own and remains inactive until it is invoked. If a function is defined but never used, that piece of code is effectively worthless. A variable in the calling function should get the returned value when a function returns a value. The function should still work without it, but the returned value will be lost, and the process may become useless. For example, if you write a function to compute the average of a set of integers and call it, it returns the average, but you don't get the returned value; there's no use in repeating the procedure.

Now it's time to call the function to calculate the volume of our tulsi plant.

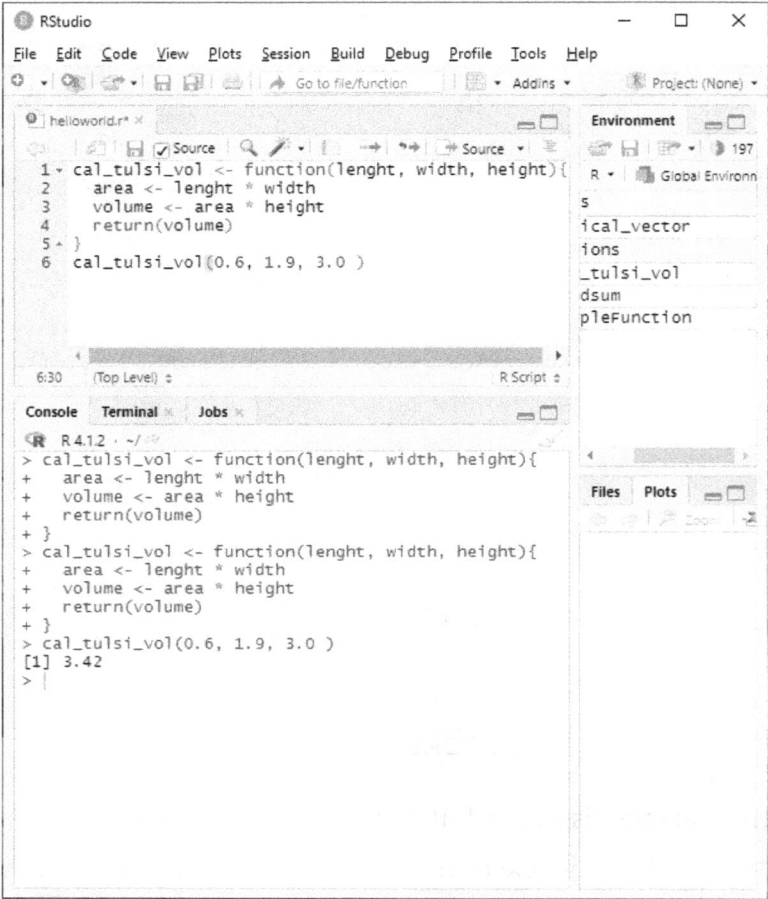

In the above picture, you can see an example of function and its execution. We assign a function to a variable "cal_tulsi_vol" inside the function, we assign the parameter (length, width, height), which is an argument, then apply some basic mathematical calculations such as multiplication. And in return, I want the answer to the last calculation, and the result is in the picture. It's essential to note that the no. of parameters in the function definition and the function call must match precisely (unless using default arguments). The parameters are also received in the same order as they were supplied during the function call.

The benefit of creating the function is we just need to change the values of the cal_tulsi_vol, and we will get a different answer. However, if you want to store the result, you need to assign it in the form of a variable. For example, using tulsi_vol as a variable and then assigning cal_tulsi_vol to it can store your answer in the script until you change it back.

In the above picture, you can see the value of tulsi_vol is saved. It was the quickest introduction to function.

Setting default arguments

After creating functions, we can set some default values to the arguments as well. We do this because sometimes we do not have complete data, so default arguments act as optional arguments to complete the data set.

Later in the book, we will learn to install packages. In those packages, there is a great use of default arguments, so we do not have to provide them. Most of the time, we want to use the general value already assigned in the functions to avoid complications. Anytime we do not provide an optional argument, the function will use the default argument in its place.

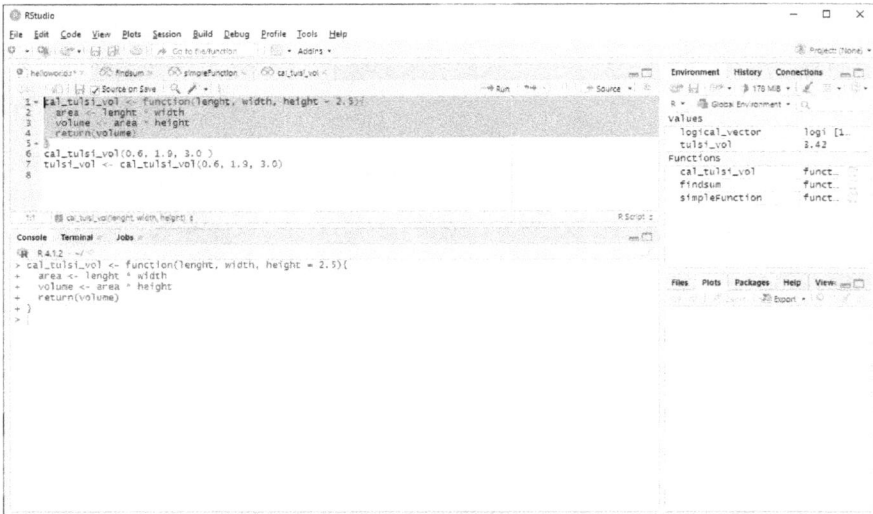

Using the previous example, I assign a value to the height argument. After that, we need to run the code to activate the function.

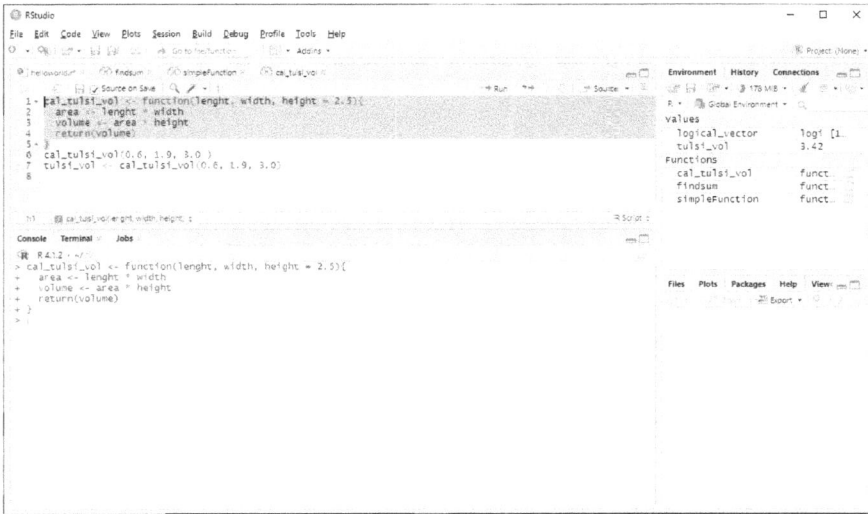

Here you can see I removed the value which was supposed to be assigned for the height argument. So my function uses the default argument to fill the missing values and gives us the result.

Named and unnamed arguments

The arguments are always assigned by their given positions. Naming the argument is necessary if you have some specific data in chronological order. For example,

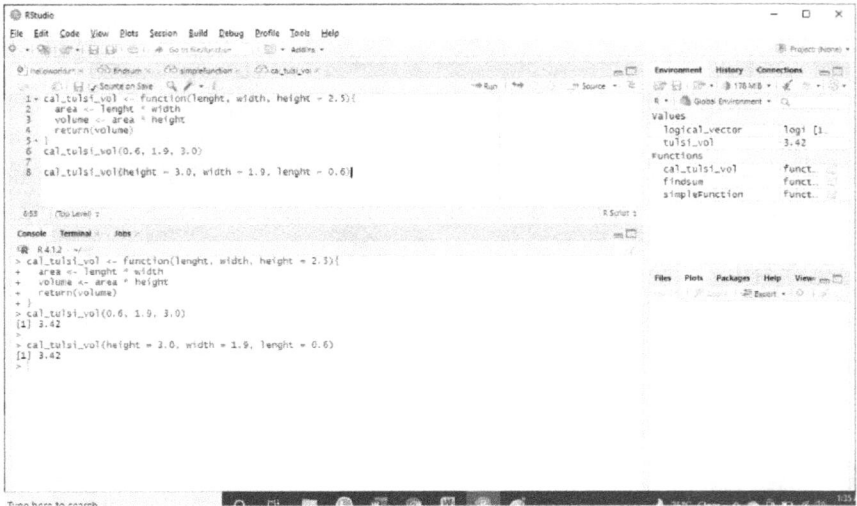

In the above picture, I named each of the arguments. Compare it to the previous picture. The benefit of naming your arguments is that you don't need to follow the order; the value will match itself instead of position. We will get the same result. Most of the coders will use unnamed/position-based arguments commonly. But in cases where remembering order is difficult, we use named arguments for the specific argument instead of altering the entire data set... It reduces the chances of error.

Combine multiple functions

Sometimes we need more than one function to perform the assigned task. Creating functions separately is tricky, but with this simple explanation, you will be able to call one function within another function effectively. It's possible to call one function from another, as well as nest one function call inside another.

In the above example, we defined another function that estimates the mass of the tulsi plant from its volume. Using est_tulsi_mass as a name for our new function, we declare a value of 2.77 * volume^0.7 this means that mass can be calculated using the equation 2.77 times 'volume' raised to p.7. lastly, return the mass to the outer program. Run this code to create a function first.

Using intermediate variables, we can combine functions to get the outcome. In the above example picture, you can see that we created a variable named tulsi_vol and assigned the output of cal_tulsi_vol. Using the same values of height, width, and length in cal_tulsi_vol will create our tulsi volume. After that, we can create a tulsi_mass variable just like before. We will call our next function in the sequence, the est_tulsi_mass, and pass the output of the previous calculations, that is, tulsi_vol. And you can see the outcome in the picture above. We get the result of 6.5508. this is the mass of the tulsi plant based on its volume.

Before moving forward, I suggest that you should practice this in RStudio as much as you can because from here, you are starting to step up to a little bit harder version of this book.

Specialized functions

You'll learn about three different types of customized user-defined R functions in this section. We'll start with "helper functions"; they are called many times by other functions (plus, it could be written within a parent function's body). After that, we'll look into "disposable" functions. That can be used as a direct parameter in another function call. Lastly, we'll study "recursive" functions or functions that call themselves.

Helper function

"R "uses their body codes to make the functions call each other frequently. A "helper" function is a word that refers to functions that are developed with the intent of assisting the computations of another Writing Function. They're proved to be a good approach to making difficult routines more readable.

You can define a "helper" function internally (inside other function descriptions) and externally (within another function description) (within the global environment).

Discarded function

Functions that can be discarded

Frequently, you'll want a function that performs a single-line operation. When using apply, for example, you'll usually only want to give a small, simple function as an argument. Discarded functions solve this problem by allowing you to declare a function for usage in a single example without having to openly create a new object in the "global environment."

Recursive Functions

Functions that are recursive

When a function calls itself, this is known as recursion. Although this method isn't widely utilized in statistical analysis, it's useful to know about this function. In this section, we will explain what it means? For a function to call itself in a simple way.

Let's say we wish to develop a "function" that accepts a "single positive" integer input n and comes back to the Fibonacci sequence's Xth term (where X=4 and X=5 correspond to the first two terms 4 and 4, separately). Previously, you used a loop to iteratively build up the Fibonacci sequence. In its place of utilizing a "loop" to send back action, a "recursive" function calls itself numerously.

Strings

A string is a collection of characters in a certain order. The character data type in R includes strings. So far, we've looked at a lot of string examples. We'll review the ideas we already know and learn a few new things about strings in this chapter.

Creating string

Throughout this chapter, we have used string many times. A string is any value between single quotes or double quotes. For example, *string <- " I am a string"* is the example of a string or *string <- 'this is also a string.'* It does not matter if we use single or double quotes; as long as we are using the same closing quote as the opening quote, our code will work properly.

What if we want to use quotes between the string?. This is also possible, If you want to include a single quote in your string, you must enclose it in double quotations, and if you want to include a double quote in your string, you must wrap it in single quotes. For example, *string <- "teacher's."*

Rules for string creation

1. Both double and single quotes should appear at the beginning and end of a string. It is impossible to combine them.

2. A string that starts and ends with a single quotation may have a double quote placed into it.

3. At the beginning and end of a string, a single quotation may be placed between double quotations.

Memorizing these rules will be easy if you keep practicing them. With the help of the following picture, you can practice the code on your Rstudio.

Manipulation of string

Now that we learned what strings are, it's time to apply some functions to the strings and manipulate their string.

String concatenating

Cat and paste are the two major functions for "concatenating" (or gluing together) one or more strings. The distinction between the two is in the manner in which their subjects return. The cat function is the first function outputs straight to the "console" screen and does not give anything technically. The "paste" function "concatenates" its arguments and gives the resulting "character string" as an "R" object. Once the outcome of a "string concatenation" has to be given to an alternative function or utilized in another method, rather than merely being shown, this is beneficial. Consider the following character string vector:

```
File   Edit   Code   View   Plots   Session   Build   Debug   Profile   Tools

  ●  ▾  ●  ▾  ●  ▾  ⊟  ⊞  ⊜  ↗  Go to file/function         ▾  Addins

  ● Untitled1* ×

    ⟲     ⊟  ☐ Source on Save    Q    ▾
    1   a= "R is"
    2   b = "easy"
    3   c ="language"
    4   paste(a,b,c)
    5
    6   paste(a,b,c, sep = '-')|




    6:24     (Top Level) ≑

  Console   Terminal    Jobs

  R  R 4.1.2 · ~/
  > a= "R is"
  > b = "easy"
  > c ="language"
  > paste(a,b,c)
  [1] "R is easy language"
  > a= "R is"
  > b = "easy"
  > c ="language"
  > paste(a,b,c)
  [1] "R is easy language"
  >
  > paste(a,b,c, sep = '-')
  [1] "R is-easy-language"
  >
```

138

In the above example, you can see that I assign variables a,b,c some values. Using the paste function, I can call them together, and we get a result of " r is easy language". This function separates the words by default by giving them one space. Let's say I don't want this spacing between the words; instead, I want a hyphen (-) in between. Using "sep" in the paste function allows me to add my desired separator.

Substring

A substring is a smaller version of a larger string. For example, if we have the text "Hello, I am a string," we can see that "I am" is a component of the string and so may be considered a substring. There are, of course, many more substring instances here. A function named substring may be used to retrieve a substring from a string.

The result of this method is a string that is a substring of the given string. Here's an R script that shows how to use concatenation and substrings:

```
Untitled1* ×
    Source on Save    Q    ⁄ ▾      → Run    ↦   ⫸ Source ▾
1   x <- "hello i am a string"
2   substr(x, start = 6, stop = 10)
3   substring(x, first = 6, last = 10)

3:1    (Top Level) ⇕                                    R Script ⇕
Console    Terminal ×    Jobs ×
R   R 4.1.2 · ~/
> substr(x, start = 6, stop = 10)
[1] " i am"
> substring(x, first = 6, last = 10)
[1] " i am"
>
```

In the above example, you can see that I sued two functions to call out the substring. The first one is *"substr"* in this function; I specified the starting and ending point using the "start" and "stop" functions. Now keep in mind that my string includes the spaces between them as well. So my substring starts after the 6th space on the string and ends before the 10th space. The second script also

140

needs to be specified by assigning "first" and "last" positions. We get the same results as we used the same parameters of the position.

There is a slew of other built-in functions that may assist with string manipulation. Let's have a look at a couple of additional features we may use.

Length of string

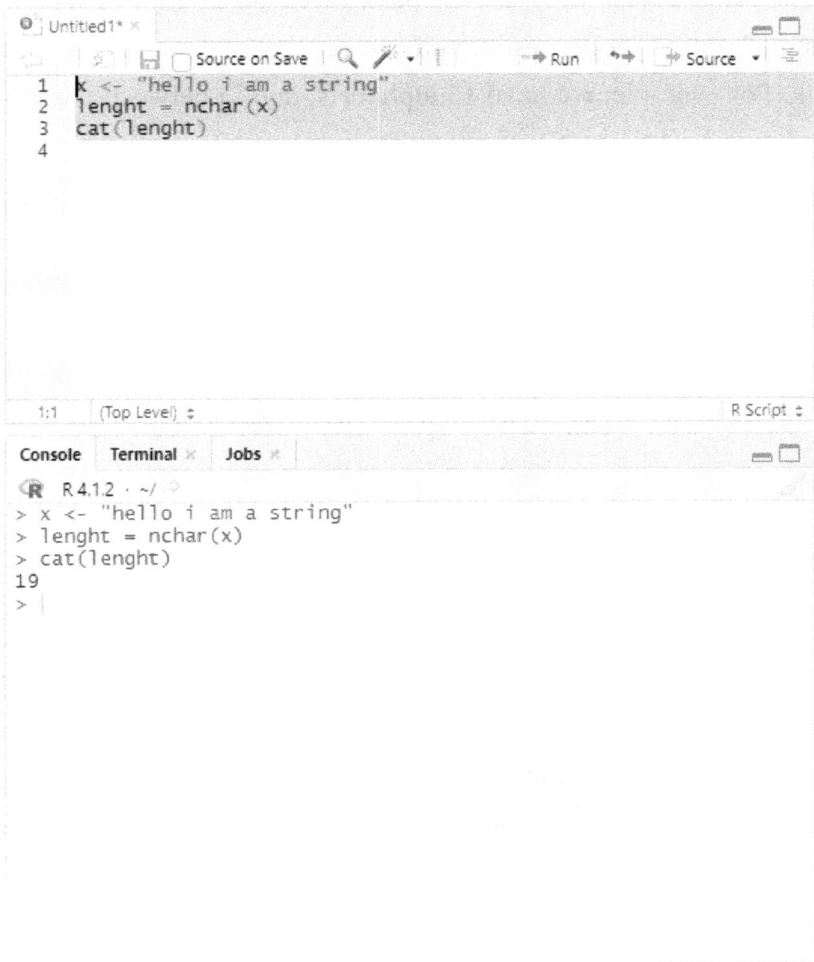

```
1  x <- "hello i am a string"
2  lenght = nchar(x)
3  cat(lenght)
4
```

Console   Terminal   Jobs

R R 4.1.2 · ~/
```
> x <- "hello i am a string"
> lenght = nchar(x)
> cat(lenght)
19
>
```

In our examples, we are using a very small amount of letters in strings. There will be large datasets when you start working that you need to handle. The length function also comes in handy in many situations. In the above example, I used "*nchar*" function to find out the length of the string. To execute this function, first, you need to allocate a string to a variable. Then you need to assign the "*nchar*" function to a variable named length or whatever you like to call it. After that, simply use the paste or cat function to display the "length" output. In the result, you can see the total spaces our string took. For example, we have 15 alphabets, and in between them, we used spacing 4 times. So our outcome came as 19.

Change the sentence case

To convert a string to upper and lower case, respectively, use the built-in methods "toupper" and "tolower".

```
Untitled1* ×
Source on Save                              Source
1  x <- "Hello I Am a String"
2  upper_case = toupper(x)
3  cat(upper_case)
4
5  x <- "hello i am a string"
6  lower_case = tolower(x)
```

For this example, I changed the sentence case of some of the alphabet. Using "*toupper*" and "*tolower*" functions, we can change the sentence case of our strings very easily. These functions are rarely used but are called miscellaneous functions for string operations.

Factors

"Factors" are categorical statistics items that we use to classify information. Consider a table that has columns such as name, age, and gender that keeps personal information about individuals. Let's have a look at the gender column. If we take this column and convert it to a vector, all we'll get is the words "Male" and "Female" repeated over and over. The distinctions between the two categories – "Male" and "Female" – are crucial. Levels are the names for these categories. In the most basic terms, if you attempt to factor a vector, the unique components from that vector will be recovered as levels. The factor () function may be used to convert a vector to a factor. Let us implement the factor function in the following example.

```
1  data <- c("doctor" , "pilot" , "doctor" ,
2            "doctor" , "engineer","pilot" , "pilot",
3            "pilot", "engineer" , "engineer")
4  #aplly the function for factor.
5  fac_data <- factor(data)
6  print(fac_data)
7
```

```
> data <- c("doctor" , "pilot" , "doctor" ,
+           "doctor" , "engineer","pilot" , "pilot",
+           "pilot", "engineer" , "engineer")
> #aplly the function for factor.
> fac_data <- factor(data)
> print(fac_data)
 [1] doctor   pilot    doctor   doctor   engineer
 [6] pilot    pilot    pilot    engineer engineer
Levels: doctor engineer pilot
>
```

As you can see, I assigned three professions to the *"data"* variable. Then applying the factor function, we create a *"fac_data"* variable, and inside the variable, we use factor and assign *"data"* to it. Then we simply print the outcome by assigning the *"fac_data"* to the print function. As a result, we get three levels of data here doctor, engineer, and pilot, respectively.

The function *"is. factor"* may be used to determine if a variable is of factor type ( ). If the supplied variable is a factor, this method will return TRUE; otherwise, it will return FALSE. For example:

```
1  data <- c("doctor" , "pilot" , "doctor" ,
2            "doctor" , "engineer","pilot" , "pilot",
3            "pilot", "engineer" , "engineer")
4  #aplly the function for factor.
5  fac_data <- factor(data)
6  print(fac_data)
7  is.factor(fac_data)
8
```

```
> data <- c("doctor" , "pilot" , "doctor" ,
+           "doctor" , "engineer","pilot" , "pilot",
+           "pilot", "engineer" , "engineer")
> #aplly the function for factor.
> fac_data <- factor(data)
> print(fac_data)
 [1] doctor    pilot     doctor    doctor    engineer
 [6] pilot     pilot     pilot     engineer  engineer
Levels: doctor engineer pilot
> is.factor(fac_data)
[1] TRUE
>
```

In the above picture, we demonstrate how we can verify if the variable is, in fact, data type or not. Using "*is.factor(fac_data)*," we can confirm that it is, in fact, a data type variable. Now you can also copy this code to your R studio, and just for example, in place of *fac_data*, just type data and see if the results come as true or false.

It will definitely come False as "*data*" is not a factor variable; it is a simple variable.

When we learn about Data Frames and File Handling in the next chapters, the use and relevance of factors will become evident.

```
Untitled1* ×
                Source on Save          Run        Source  ▾
1   simpson <- data.frame( "name" = c("jhon", "nida", "steve
2                          "age" = c(25,44,66), "height" = (
3                          "occupation" = c("Student", "Emp"
4   print(simpson)
5   data.frame(simpson
6       ) [1 ]

5:1    (Top Level) ÷                                R Script ÷

Console   Terminal ×   Jobs ×
R   R 4.1.2 · ~/
> data.frame(simpson
+       ) [1 ]
     name
1   jhon
2   nida
3 steve
>
```

Chapter 8

Data Frames

A "data frame" is just like a worksheet, a collection of facts organised within a series of named columns and rows. Effectively, a data frame can be seen as the next step up in the organisational hierarchy of data structures. Much like a vector is a collection of individual data points, a data frame is simply a collection of vectors. Just like how you used the combine function to create your vectors, you can produce the function data—frame () to make a "data frame" through vectors.

Using data.frame() is extremely similar to using c(), the biggest difference is that we must name each column (vector) in our data frame as such:

```
> data.frame(column_1 = vector1,
column_2 = vector2)
```

You can use your newly created vectors to create a data frame which we will call "Simpson."

```
simpson <- data.frame( "name" =
c("jhon", "nida", "steve"), "age" =
c(25,44,66), "height" =
c(4.9,7.2,5.4),  "occupation" =
c("Student", "Employed", "Student"))
print(simpson
        )
```

Notice that in the example above, we have nested the combine function within the data frame function. This allows us to create a vector specifically for this data frame. Nesting functions is an extremely handy practice that you will find yourself often doing throughout your R programming career.

Using the print() function, let's take a gaze at the new "data frame." "print()" function simply opens an information structure to inspect its contents visually. To execute this function, you can simply type print(Simpson) into the console. You can also access this same command by double-clicking the data structure you wish to view in the environment pane in RStudio. Whichever method you have chosen, RStudio will have opened the Simpson data frame like such:

You've created a data frame containing three persons' first names, ages in years, heights, and occupations. The item returned should explain why vectors were supplied to the data. Vectors that have different dimensions would not make sense in this context; therefore frame must be of equal length. If you supply "data. frame" vectors of uneven lengths to equal the longest vector, R will reuse any lesser vectors, potentially tossing our "data" off and assigning numbers to the incorrect variable. The console is supplied with "data frames" in the form of columns and rows, like matrixes rather than a named list. This intuitive worksheet format makes reading and manipulating data sets a breeze. In a data frame, each row is referred to as documentation, and every column individually is referred to as a "variable."

Notes:

a. A data frame's columns should all have the exact same length. There will be an error if any of the columns do not have the same amount of items. Let's change the initial code in this area so that the nation column only has two values instead of three.

b. The names of the vector variables are automatically converted to column names.

c. You may add custom names to columns by generating a vector of column names and setting it as follows:

```
Name ("data frame") = <vector of column
name>
```

Retrieving Data from Data Frames

In the above example, we made some data for rainfall in mm for different cities in Europe. Now we will practice using this data as sample data for this book.

Rows, columns, and individual items may all be accessed while working with data frames. All of these options will be considered in the following part.

Rows

By selecting row and column index points, you may extract sections of the data (much as with a matrix

```
"rainfall <- data.frame("months"=c("jan",
"fab", "mar","apr",

"may","jun","jul","aug","sep",

"oct","nov","dec"),
"rain in mm" =
c(28.1,27.7,95.6,63.8,18.2,11.4

,49.6,39.9,13.1,63.8,11.9,73.4),
"city"= c("barlin", "madrid", "rome",
"paris",
          "vienna","warsaw", "hamburg",
"budapest",
            "barcelona", "munich","milan",
"sofia" ))"
print(rainfall)
```

Using the above script, you will be able to create the same data in your Rstudio. The following syntax may be used to obtain a whole row (including all columns).

```
<name of data frame> [3,]. For example.
Rainfall [3,]
```

This will call the third row of the data. For example, see the
following picture.

```
 1  rainfall <- data.frame  ("city"= c("barlin", "madrid", "rome", "paris",
 2                              "vienna","warsaw", "hamburg", "budapest",
 3                              "barcelona", "munich","milan", "sofia" ),
 4                    "rain in mm" = c(28.1,27.7,95.6,63.8,18.2,11.4
 5                              ,49.6,39.9,13.1,63.8,11.9,73.4),
 6                    "months"=c("jan" ,"fab", "mar","apr",
 7                              "may","jun","jul","aug","sep",
 8                              "oct","nov","dec"))
 9  print(rainfall)
10  rainfall[3,]
11
```

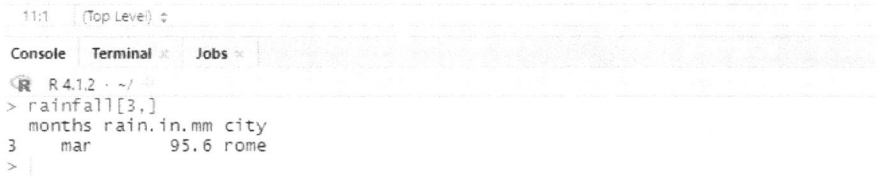

11:1   (Top Level) ⬦

Console   Terminal   Jobs

```
R  R 4.1.2 · ~/
> rainfall[3,]
  months rain.in.mm city
3    mar      95.6 rome
>
```

Unless you intend to display the third row directly, this will return
the third row as a list of values; therefore, there should be a variable
to accept it.

Different methods can be used to access selective rows. If you need
to access rows 3 through 6, do it as follows:

```
<name of data frame> [3:6,]. For example.
Rainfall [3:6,]
```

```
 1  rainfall <- data.frame    ("city"= c("barlin", "madrid", "rome", "paris",
 2                             "vienna","warsaw", "hamburg", "budapest",
 3                             "barcelona", "munich","milan", "sofia" ),
 4                  "rain in mm" = c(28.1,27.7,95.6,63.8,18.2,11.4
 5                             ,49.6,39.9,13.1,63.8,11.9,73.4),
 6                  "months"=c("jan" ,"fab", "mar","apr",
 7                             "may","jun","jul","aug","sep",
 8                             "oct","nov","dec"))
 9  print(rainfall)
10  rainfall[3:6,]
11  |
```

11:1   (Top Level) ⧎

Console   Terminal   Jobs

R R 4.1.2 · ~/

```
> rainfall[3:6,]
  months rain.in.mm    city
3    mar       95.6    rome
4    apr       63.8   paris
5    may       18.2  vienna
6    jun       11.4  warsaw
>
```

If only the third and ninth rows need to be accessible, perform these steps:

```
<name of data frame> [3:6,]. For example.
Rainfall [c(3,9),]
```

```
    1  rainfall <- data.frame   ("city"= c("barlin", "madrid", "rome", "paris",
    2                             "vienna","warsaw", "hamburg", "budapest",
    3                             "barcelona", "munich","milan", "sofia" ),
    4               "rain in mm" = c(28.1,27.7,95.6,63.8,18.2,11.4
    5                             ,49.6,39.9,13.1,53.8,11.9,73.4),
    6               "months"=c("jan" ,"fab", "mar","apr",
    7                             "may","jun","jul","aug","sep",
    8                             "oct","nov","dec"))
    9  print(rainfall)
   10  rainfall[c(3,9),]
   11  |
```

11:1   (Top Level) ¢

Console   Terminal   Jobs

```
R  R 4.1.2 · ~/
> rainfall[c(3,4),]
  months rain.in.mm   city
3    mar      95.6   rome
4    apr      63.8  paris
> rainfall[c(3,9),]
  months rain.in.mm        city
3    mar      95.6        rome
9    sep      13.1  barcelona
>
```

Special values

Many circumstances in R need the use of special values. While a data collection has omitted numbers or a nearly endless observation is computed, for example, the program includes certain special terminology reserved for these scenarios. In vectors, arrays, and other data structures, we can use these special values to indicate aberrant or omitted values.

Infinite numbers

R establishes upper and lower bounds on how extreme a number may be before the program is unable to correctly denote it. When an observation is too big for "R" to handle, it's assumed to be "infinite." Naturally, the arithmetic idea of infinity doesn't equate to a precise observation—all "R" needs to do is identify a risky endpoint. The exact endpoint value differs by the system and is

153

influenced in part by the extent of RAM available to "R." The value is usually denoted by the case-sensitive special object Inf. Inf can only be used with numeric vectors since it represents a numeric value. To put it to the test, let's make some objects.

```
1   list <- Inf
2   list
3   uni <- c(3401,Inf,3.1,-555,Inf,43)
4   uni
5   col <- 70000^100
6   col
7   |
```

```
> list <- Inf
> list
[1] Inf
> uni <- c(3401,Inf,3.1,-555,Inf,43)
> uni
[1] 3401.0    Inf    3.1 -555.0    Inf   43.0
> col <- 70000^100
> col
[1] Inf
>
```

We've created a single instance of an infinite value in the form of an object list. We've similarly created a "numeric" vector, uni, with two endless components and then multiplied 70 thousand by 100 in col to get a value R considers infinite.

NaN

In some cases, expressing the outcome of computation using a no. or information, or -Inf is tough. In R, these difficult-to-quantify unusual values are referred to as NaN or Not a Number.

"NaN" values, like infinite values, are solely connected with numerical observations. Although it is probable to declare or include a "NaN" value explicitly, this is an uncommon occurrence.

```
1  list <- NaN
2  list
3  uni <- c(NaN, 60.3,NaN,79898.54,-Inf,45)
4  uni
5
6  |
```

```
6:1    (Top Level) ¢                                    R Script

Console   Terminal    Jobs

R   R 4.1.2 · ~/
> list <- NaN
> list
[1] NaN
> uni <- c(NaN, 60.3,NaN,79898.54,-Inf,45)
> uni
[1]       NaN      60.30       NaN  79898.54       -Inf
[6]     45.00
>
```

Attempting to do a computation that is impossible to accomplish with the provided data usually results in "NaN."

```
1  -Inf+Inf
2
3  0/0
4  |
```

Console   Terminal   Jobs

```
R  R 4.1.2 · ~/
> -Inf+Inf
[1] NaN
> 0/0
[1] NaN
>
```

If we try to withdraw infinite demonstrations in any manner, the outcome will be "NaN." As negative and positive infinity cannot be understood in that numeric sense, the first line won't return zero; therefore, you'll receive "NaN" instead.

When you divide Inf by itself, the same thing occurs. Furthermore, despite the fact that is dividing a non-zero number by zero yields negative or positive infinity, dividing zero by zero yields NaN. It's worth noting that any mathematical process that involves NaN will just produce NaN.

```
1  NaN+1
2  7+4*(7-8)/0
3  10.223^(-Inf+Inf)|
```

```
3:18    (Top Level) ÷                                    R Script ÷
Console   Terminal   Jobs

R   R 4.1.2 · ~/
> NaN+1
[1] NaN
> 7+4*(7-8)/0
[1] -Inf
> 10.223^(-Inf+Inf)
[1] NaN
>
```

When you add 1 to "not a number" in the first line, you get NaN... The outcome of the second line is equally "NaN" because the (4-4)/0 is plainly 0/0. Because -Inf/Inf yields NaN in the third line, the remainder of the computation yields "NaN" as well. This begins to show how "NaN" or endless values could appear inadvertently. If we fail to take care or avoid o/o from occurring in a function where numerous values are supplied to a fixed computation, the code will return "NaN."

NA

Data sets with missing values are common in statistical analysis. For example, a person taking part in a survey cannot reply to a certain topic, or a scholar can mistakenly write down some results from an investigation.

It's critical to identify and handle missing values so that the remainder of the data may be used. NA, which stands for Not Available, is a typical special word in R for missing data.

NA and NaN entries are not the same thing. Missing values may occur for any form of observation, but NaN is exclusively utilized for numeric operations. As a result, NAs may be found in both numerical and non-numerical contexts.

NULL

Finally, you'll examine the null value, denoted by the letter "NULL." This observation is often used to create an "empty" object that is distinct from a "missing" object defined with "NA." "NA" clearly signifies an existent place that may be accessed and/or rewritten if required; NULL, on the other hand, does not.

COERCION, TYPE AND CLASSES:

Many of the core elements of the R language for expressing, storing, and manipulating data have already been covered. In the following lesson, we'll learn how we can formally differentiate among various types of structure and values, as well as learn some easy conversion cases.

ATTRIBUTES

Every "R" entity we write has extra info on the entity's nature—the characteristics of the entity related to this extra material. You've already seen a few characteristics. You used dim to find the lengths attribute of a matrix. We used different levels to acquire a factor's levels property in Section 4.3.1. In Section 5.1.2, it was also said that names might be used to acquire the names of a list's members, and in Section 6.1.3, an attribute can be used to annotate the result of using na.omit.

In general, qualities are classified as either explicit or implicit.

The user can see explicit characteristics right away, but R determines implicit attributes internally. The "attributes" function that accepts any entity and produces a "named list" may be used to print obvious attributes for a given entity. Consider the three-dimensional matrix below:

Chapter 9

Working with Data

Installing Packages

Thus far, through the use of this book, you have performed quite a few different functions and calculations within base R. You have successfully assigned names to various objects in your R environment with <-, programmed your first vectors using c(), created data frames with data.frame(), and you've analyzed your objects, vectors, and data frames with both class() and view (). By this point in your R programming journey, you've no doubt learned just how powerful of a programming language R could be. While these are only a few of the many functions to be found in base R, this book would not be helpful if it did not introduce you to R packages.

More specialized functions may be significantly simpler and more efficient to program when working through particular challenges. This is where R packages come into play. A package in R is a collection of R functions created to solve specific problems either not included in base R or in more simplified code than in base R. Within the CRAN. There are thousands of R packages for many different R programming needs. The basic R functions are used to install and load R packages such as installed. packages() and library(). You can also install many CRAN packages via the Packages tab found in the Viewer Pane.

When installing a new package to your R programming session, you will first execute the install. Packages ("name of the package you want to install")into your R console. With this book's emphasis on data analysis, few packages prove to be as useful as the Tidyverse. Let us install the Tidyverse now as an example.

```
> install.packages("tidyverse")
```

Note: You may have noticed that due to the many functions found within the Tidyverse, its installation may take more time to execute than any of the functions you have executed previously.

Once your Tidyverse package has successfully been installed, it is time that you load it into your current R session. This is done via the library() function. Much like the install.packages() function, the library() function's syntax is written as library("name of the package you want to load"). Let's again use the Tidyverse as our example package to load in.

```
"> library("tidyverse")
-- Attaching packages ----------------------
----- tidyverse 1.3.1 -
v ggplot2 3.3.5      v purrr    0.3.4
v tibble  3.1.4      v dplyr    1.0.7
v tidyr   1.1.3      v stringr  1.4.0
v readr   2.0.1      v forcats  0.5.1
```

```
-- Conflicts ---------------------------
tidyverse_conflicts() -
x dplyr::filter() masks stats::filter()
x dplyr::lag()    masks stats::lag()
```

Warning message:

```
package 'tidyverse' was built under R
version 4.1.2"
```

When finished, you will notice that two base R functions have effectively been replaced by functions from the dplyr package. These two conflicts are simply just warnings informing you of these changes. Your console will also list the eight Tidyverse packages now loaded into your R programming session.

Enter the Tidyverse

The Tidyverse is a unique R package in the way that it is a package of packages designed around the data analysis process. When installing the Tidyverse to your R programming session, you are, in reality, installing the packages ggplot2, dplyr, readr, tidyr, purr, Tibble, stringr, and forecast. While you could individually install each of these packages, installing them via the Tidyverse narrows what would otherwise be 16 lines of code down to two.

Now that you have successfully installed the Tidyverse and have an understanding of basic R programming and basic data cleaning and organization, it is time to begin diving deeper into the world of data transformation with R. As stated in the previous chapter; the Tidyverse is an R package by the name dplyr. Dplyr is a set of data analysis functions based on data manipulation. This makes dplyr an

162

excellent package for sorting, filtering, and manipulating your data to gain a better understanding of the story hidden within it.

Manipulating Data

Dplyr comes built-in with many powerful data manipulation functions. In this book, the most common six data manipulation functions will be discussed. These functions are filter(), select(), summarize(), arrange(), mutate(), and group_by(). Each one of these functions is incredibly useful in quickly navigating through data to learn more about what it is you are analyzing.

Filtering data with filter()

As you have likely guessed, filter() is a data manipulation function that allows one to quickly filter through a data frame based on a specified value. With the filter() function, the standard syntax pattern you will follow looks like this:

```
> filter("Data frame you are starting with",
"column you are filtering" == "filter
criteria")
```

In the Simpson data frame you created earlier in this book, a use for the filter() would be to filter all of the characters who are female. In order to do this with the filter() function, you would type this line of code into the console:

```
> filter(Simpsons, boy == "FALSE")
      name age height    boy occupation
1    Lisa   8   4.12 FALSE    Student
2   Marge  34   8.50 FALSE  Homemaker
3 Maggie   1   2.23 FALSE       None
```

Notice that we use the double = symbol to inform are that we need every observation where the value in the "boy" column is "FALSE."

What if we want to return all of the characters who are not boys?

```
> filter(Simpson, boy != "TRUE")
    name age height   boy occupation
1   Lisa   8   4.12 FALSE     Student
2  Marge  34   8.50 FALSE   Homemaker
3 Maggie   1   2.23 FALSE        None
```

Here you will see that we use the != to denote that we are looking for R to return all the observations where the value in the "boy" column does not equal "TRUE."

Now it is important to note that while these two lines of code produce the same result when filtering through the "boy" column of the Simpson data frame, the two lines of code are asking two completely different things of R. Yes, it doesn't necessarily make any difference in this example, let's look at these lines of code when applied to another column in the Simpsons. Let's try filter() on the occupation column to demonstrate the use of !=.

```
> filter(simpson, occupation != "Student")
    name age height   boy occupation
1  Homer  36   6.00  TRUE   Employed
2  Marge  34   8.50 FALSE  Homemaker
3 Maggie   1   2.23 FALSE       None
```

Being able to filter for values that are equal or not equal to a specified value is not the only way you are able to make use of dplyr's filter() function. The filter() function can also be used as a tool to filter out values that are greater than or less than a specified value. This can be done simply by replacing the != or == with either the greater-than (>) or less-than (<) symbol. You can also use >= and <= while looking for values that are higher than, less than, or equal to the value you provide. Not only this, but you are able to filter for more than one argument at a time. What if you wanted to find out which characters among the Simpson data frame are not only female but are younger than 20 years old?

```
> filter(simpson, boy == "FALSE", age < 20)
    name age height    boy occupation
1   Lisa   8   4.12 FALSE    Student
2 Maggie   1   2.23 FALSE       None
```

Being able to filter through a column based on a singular value is very useful, but what if you need to filter for two different values at the same time? Dplyr's filter() function has been designed knowing that such situations will come up and will need to be solved. For problems like these, you can use the & and | symbols. "&" meaning "and" and "|" meaning "or."

So what if you wanted to find the characters who are older than 20 years old, but you also want to pull the characters who are younger than 10? You would use the | symbol in this way:

```
> filter(Simpson, age > 20 | age < 10)
    name age height    boy occupation
1  Homer  36   6.00  TRUE   Employed
2   Lisa   8   4.12 FALSE    Student
3  Marge  34   8.50 FALSE  Homemaker
4 Maggie   1   2.23 FALSE       None
```

Similarly, if you wanted to pull the characters whose occupation is Student and is 10 years old, you would execute this line of code:

```
> filter(Simpson, occupation == "Student" &
age == 10)
  name age height  boy occupation
1 Bart  10      4 TRUE    Student
```

Pulling specific columns with select()

So you have successfully used the filter() function to filter out values from your data frame to find specific observations that match your criteria. But what if you wish to filter out entire columns from your data frame? What if you only wish to view the character name and their height from the Simpsons data frame? Maybe you wish to assign these two columns to their own data frame. This is where the dplyr's select() function comes in handy. The syntax for the select()function follows a very similar pattern as the filter() function. You will find that many of the functions in dplyr follow a close pattern. For the select() function, it looks like this:

```
> select("Data frame you are starting with,"
"column you want to pull")
```

Back to the original question about creating a data frame that consists only of the character names and their height. Using the assignment skills, you have learned early on and the select()function, let us create this data frame by selecting the name and age columns and calling it something like character_height.

166

```
> character_height <- select(simpson, name,
height)
> character_height
    name height
1    Bart   4.00
2   Homer   6.00
3    Lisa   4.12
4   Marge   8.50
5  Maggie   2.23
```

An important note about the lines of code written above. You will notice the line that states, "#Let's take a look at the character_height data frame." This line is simply a comment on the next line of code. Comments are a very handy method of leaving notes and descriptions about your code for others or yourself. Comments, while useful in the console alone, will really prove their worth once you begin working in R scripts. This book will go into more detail on comments and R scripts in an upcoming chapter.

Adding values with mutate()

While the Simpson data frame you have created is handy and contains a bit of information. What if you wanted to add columns to the data frame? What if you felt it was important to have a column that allowed you to have each character's age in dog years? This is one of the problems you are able to solve with the dplyr mutate() function. The mutate() function can create these new columns based on vectors or simply other columns found within your data frame. The mutate() functions syntax is seen as such:

```
> mutate("Data frame you are starting with",
"New column" = "criteria of new column")
```

In the dog years problem listed above, you could use the mutate()
function to add the new column by multiplying each character's age
value by seven as such:

```
> mutate(Simpson, dog_years = age * 7)
     name age height    boy occupation
dog_years
1    Bart  10   4.00   TRUE    Student          70
2   Homer  36   6.00   TRUE   Employed         252
3    Lisa   8   4.12  FALSE    Student          56
4   Marge  34   8.50  FALSE  Homemaker         238
5  Maggie   1   2.23  FALSE       None           7
```

You can also use mutate() to add columns with new vectors.

```
> mutate(simpson, family_role = c("Son",
"Father", "Daughter", "Mother", "Daughter"))
     name age height    boy occupation
family_role
1    Bart  10   4.00   TRUE    Student        Son
2   Homer  36   6.00   TRUE   Employed     Father
3    Lisa   8   4.12  FALSE    Student   Daughter
4   Marge  34   8.50  FALSE  Homemaker     Mother
5  Maggie   1   2.23  FALSE       None   Daughter
```

Rearranging columns of arranging ()

What if, when working with your Simpson data frame, you decide
that it would be much easier to read and understand the data if the
columns were listed in another order? How about if the characters
were listed in order by their age or by their name alphabetically?
These are exactly what dplyr's arrange() function allows you to
accomplish. Following the same pattern as the rest of the dplyr
functions' syntax, arrange() can be written like such:

```
> arrange("Data frame you are starting
with," "column to sort by")
```

Let us take the example of sorting the Simpson data frame by the age of each character. We can do this by using the arrange() function on the age column like so:

```
> arrange(Simpson, age)
      name age height    boy occupation
1 Maggie   1   2.23 FALSE       None
2   Lisa   8   4.12 FALSE    Student
3   Bart  10   4.00  TRUE    Student
4  Marge  34   8.50 FALSE  Homemaker
5  Homer  36   6.00  TRUE   Employed
```

But what if you wanted the characters arranged by oldest to youngest as opposed to the youngest to oldest method printed above? When using the arrange() function, R will assume that the column you wish to arrange will be sorted in ascending order. In order to reverse this, you can simply nest the function desc() within the arrange() function. To achieve the reverse arrangement of the data frame shown above, you would apply the desc() function on the age column as so:

```
> arrange(Simpson, desc(age))
      name age height    boy occupation
1  Homer  36   6.00  TRUE   Employed
2  Marge  34   8.50 FALSE  Homemaker
3   Bart  10   4.00  TRUE    Student
4   Lisa   8   4.12 FALSE    Student
5 Maggie   1   2.23 FALSE       None
```

It is also worth noting that you are able to sort by more than one column with the arrange() function. To do so, you simply add another column argument into the function. R will then use each column argument after the first as a method of breaking ties in the prior arrangement. Remember, R will assign priority to the arrangements based on the order they are written within the line of code.

Analyzing Large Datasets

Thus far in your data journey, you have been analyzing the Simpson data frame that you created. The Simpson data frame has been an extremely useful example for learning and becoming more comfortable with writing lines of code to analyze data in R. However, with only 5 observations of 5 variables, you may have asked yourself why not just use view () to look at the entire data frame and quickly gather all the information at once? It is important to mention that R was designed for working with data frames hundreds of thousands of times larger than your Simpson data frames. As such, from this point on, The Palmer Penguins data package will be used. For its examples moving forward in order to demonstrate the true power of programming in the R language.

The Palmer Penguins data package is an R package that consists of two datasets that contain data about various different penguins collected by "Dr. Kristen Gorman" and the "Palmer Station" from "Antarctica LTER." They are also members of the "Long Term Ecological Research" Network. The data for Palmer Penguins is very useful for learning to analyze data with R due to its cleanliness

170

and not overly large size. Since the Palmer Penguins data package is available via the CRAN, you are able to easily install required datasets into the R programming session in the same way you did the Tidyverse.

```
> install.packages("palmerpenguins")
```

WARNING: Rtools is needed to generate R packages, but it isn't installed yet. Before continuing, please download and install the relevant version of Rtools.

```
https://cran.rstudio.com/bin/windows/Rtools/
Installing the package into 'C:/...'
(as 'lib' is unspecified)
trying URL
'https://cran.rstudio.com/bin/windows/contri
b/4.1/palmerpenguins_0.1.0.zip'
Content type 'application/zip' length
3003088 bytes (2.9 MB)
downloaded 2.9 MB

package 'palmerpenguins' successfully
unpacked, and MD5 sums checked

The downloaded binary packages are in
    C:\...

> library(palmerpenguins)
Warning message:
package 'palmerpenguins' was built under R
version 4.1.2
```

Now that you have installed and loaded the Palmer Penguins data package into your R session, let's check out the two datasets included in the package; "penguins" and "penguins_raw."

You quickly understand your data.

When working with large datasets, it can be incredibly daunting trying to figure out what information you have available to you and where to even begin your investigation. This is especially tricky when working with a dataset in which you have no prior experience. Thankfully, R has a few handy functions which allow you to gather a fast understanding of what all information can be found within the dataset. These functions are the head(), tail(), colnames() and glimpse().

Now, you have already used view () in the past to open up an entire data frame, but what if you just would like to take a peek into the data. The head() and tail() are excellent functions to do so. With both of these functions, R will report back a small sample summary of six observations. The difference between the two functions is that head() will populate the first six observations, while tail() will populate the final six observations. Let's test them both out with the penguins_raw dataset.

```
> head(penguins_raw)
# A tibble: 6 x 17
   studyName `Sample Number` Species
       Region Island  Stage  `Individual ID`
 `Clutch Complet~ `Date Egg` `Culmen Length ~
    <chr>                 <dbl> <chr>      <chr>
 <chr>    <chr>   <chr>         <chr>
       <date>                  <dbl>
```

```
1 PAL0708                    1 Adelie Pe~
Anvers Torger~ Adult~ N1A1              Yes
    2007-11-11              39.1
2 PAL0708                    2 Adelie Pe~
Anvers Torger~ Adult~ N1A2              Yes
    2007-11-11              39.5
3 PAL0708                    3 Adelie Pe~
Anvers Torger~ Adult~ N2A1              Yes
    2007-11-16              40.3
4 PAL0708                    4 Adelie Pe~
Anvers Torger~ Adult~ N2A2              Yes
    2007-11-16              NA
5 PAL0708                    5 Adelie Pe~
Anvers Torger~ Adult~ N3A1              Yes
    2007-11-16              36.7
6 PAL0708                    6 Adelie Pe~
Anvers Torger~ Adult~ N3A2              Yes
    2007-11-16              39.3
# ... with 7 more variables: Culmen Depth
(mm) <dbl>, Flipper Length (mm) <dbl>, Body
Mass (g) <dbl>, Sex <chr>,
#   Delta 15 N (o/oo) <dbl>, Delta 13 C
(o/oo) <dbl>, Comments <chr>


> tail(penguins_raw)
# A tibble: 6 x 17
  studyName `Sample Number` Species
    Region Island Stage  `Individual ID`
`Clutch Complet~ `Date Egg` `Culmen Length ~
  <chr>               <dbl> <chr>       <chr>
<chr>  <chr>  <chr>       <chr>
    <date>              <dbl>
1 PAL0910              63 Chinstrap ~ Anvers
Dream  Adult~ N98A1        Yes
    2009-11-19              45.7
```

```
2 PAL0910              64 Chinstrap ~ Anvers
Dream  Adult~ N98A2         Yes
       2009-11-19          55.8
3 PAL0910              65 Chinstrap ~ Anvers
Dream  Adult~ N99A1         No
       2009-11-21          43.5
4 PAL0910              66 Chinstrap ~ Anvers
Dream  Adult~ N99A2         No
       2009-11-21          49.6
5 PAL0910              67 Chinstrap ~ Anvers
Dream  Adult~ N100A1        Yes
       2009-11-21          50.8
6 PAL0910              68 Chinstrap ~ Anvers
Dream  Adult~ N100A2        Yes
       2009-11-21          50.2
# ... with 7 more variables: Culmen Depth
(mm) <dbl>, Flipper Length (mm) <dbl>, Body
Mass (g) <dbl>, Sex <chr>,
#   Delta 15 N (o/oo) <dbl>, Delta 13 C
(o/oo) <dbl>, Comments <chr>
```

You will notice that at the top of your output when executing both the head() and tail() functions are the line "A tibble: 6 x 17". What this means is that your output is in the form of a table as opposed to a data frame and that this table consists of 6 rows and 17 columns. Without diving too deep into the differences between a tibble and a data frame, a tibble can be easily understood as the simplified modern version of a data frame. For more information on tibbles and the tibble package found in the Tidyverse, you can check out the Helpful Resources section of chapter 6.

Another useful peeking tool is the function colnames(). Running the colnames() function shows us simply the names of each column found within a dataset. When used with the penguins_raw data set, R will print out the names of each of the 17 columns. This can be an excellent way to gather information without being overwhelmed by anything more than the names of the columns of a dataset.

```
>colnames(penguins_raw)
 [1] "studyName"            "Sample Number"
 [3] "Species"              "Region"
 [5] "Island"               "Stage"
 [7] "Individual ID"    "Clutch Completion"
 [9] "Date Egg"            "Culmen Length (mm)"
[11] "Culmen Depth (mm)"  "Flipper Length
(mm)"
[13] "Body Mass (g)"         "Sex"
[15] "Delta 15 N (o/oo)"   "Delta 13 C
(o/oo)"
[17] "Comments"
```

Finally, we have the glimpse() function. The glimpse() function is, much like head() and tail(), a great option for taking a peek into an unfamiliar dataset and gaining a lot of knowledge as to what information hides within. Unlike the head() and tail() functions, however, glimpse() will not print out any observations from the dataset in the form of a "table" or "data frame." What glimpse() does is inform you of how many individual rows and columns there are while displaying the names and class of each column, plus a sample of the individual values of each column. Because of the glimpse() function's ability to quickly display so much information in an easy-to-read manner, glimpse() is, in this book's view, one of the most powerful and useful functions for information gathering. Let us try it out with the penguins_raw dataset.

```
> glimpse(penguins_raw)
Rows: 344
Columns: 17
$ studyName             <chr> "PAL0708",
"PAL0708", "PAL0708", "PAL0708", "PAL0708",
"PAL0708", "PAL0708", "PAL0708", "~
$ `Sample Number`       <dbl> 1, 2, 3, 4, 5,
6, 7, 8, 9, 10, 11, 12, 13, 14, 15, 16, 17,
18, 19, 20, 21, 22, 23, 24, 25~
$ Species               <chr> "Adelie
Penguin (Pygoscelis adeliae)", "Adelie
Penguin (Pygoscelis adeliae)", "Adelie Pen~
$ Region                <chr> "Anvers",
"Anvers", "Anvers", "Anvers", "Anvers",
"Anvers", "Anvers", "Anvers", "Anvers",~
$ Island                <chr> "Torgersen",
"Torgersen", "Torgersen", "Torgersen",
"Torgersen", "Torgersen", "Torgersen"~
$ Stage                 <chr> "Adult, 1 Egg
Stage", "Adult, 1 Egg Stage", "Adult, 1 Egg
Stage", "Adult, 1 Egg Stage", "~
$ `Individual ID`       <chr> "N1A1",
"N1A2", "N2A1", "N2A2", "N3A1", "N3A2",
"N4A1", "N4A2", "N5A1", "N5A2", "N6A1", "~
$ `Clutch Completion`   <chr> "Yes", "Yes",
"Yes", "Yes", "Yes", "Yes", "No", "No",
"Yes", "Yes", "Yes", "Yes", "Yes", ~
$ `Date Egg`            <date> 2007-11-11,
2007-11-11, 2007-11-16, 2007-11-16, 2007-11-
16, 2007-11-16, 2007-11-15, 2007~
$ `Culmen Length (mm)`  <dbl> 39.1, 39.5,
40.3, NA, 36.7, 39.3, 38.9, 39.2, 34.1,
42.0, 37.8, 37.8, 41.1, 38.6, 34.6, 3~
$ `Culmen Depth (mm)`   <dbl> 18.7, 17.4,
18.0, NA, 19.3, 20.6, 17.8, 19.6, 18.1,
20.2, 17.1, 17.3, 17.6, 21.2, 21.1, 1~
```

```
$ `Flipper Length (mm)` <dbl> 181, 186, 195,
NA, 193, 190, 181, 195, 193, 190, 186, 180,
182, 191, 198, 185, 195, 197, ~
$ `Body Mass (g)`        <dbl> 3750, 3800,
3250, NA, 3450, 3650, 3625, 4675, 3475,
4250, 3300, 3700, 3200, 3800, 4400, 3~
$ Sex                   <chr> "MALE",
"FEMALE", "FEMALE", NA, "FEMALE", "MALE",
"FEMALE", "MALE", NA, NA, NA, NA, "FEMA~
$ `Delta 15 N (o/oo)`   <dbl> NA, 8.94956,
8.36821, NA, 8.76651, 8.66496, 9.18718,
9.46060, NA, 9.13362, 8.63243, NA, N~
$ `Delta 13 C (o/oo)`   <dbl> NA, -24.69454,
-25.33302, NA, -25.32426, -25.29805, -
25.21799, -24.89958, NA, -25.09368, ~
$ Comments              <chr> "Not enough
blood for isotopes.", NA, NA, "Adult not
sampled.", NA, NA, "Nest never obser~
```

Using R Scripts to write code

As you have seen in the previous section, the glimpse(), head(), and tail() functions are three excellent methods of gathering a quick understanding of your data. Before we move forward in your learning process, Let's introduce you to the great tool known as R scripts. While you are able to use the console to write all of your code, you have surely found it to be rather clunky and cumbersome when writing multiple lines of code at once. Even worse, if you make a mistake in your code while writing in the console or need to save your work for later.

To create an R script in RStudio, you can simply go into the file menu and, under the "new file" tab, select "R script." Or alternatively, you can make use of the keyboard shortcut "Ctrl +

Shift + N" on "Windows" or "Cmd + Shift + N" on "macOS." You will then notice that RStudio has opened up the R script in a new window pane above the console.

When working in an R script, all you need to do is type out your lines of code into the script and select the run button in the top right of the R script pane when you want to run your code. If you wish only to run a special section of your R script, you simply highlight the previous section of code prior to selecting the run button. You will notice that by running an R script, RStudio effectively just copies your script into the console and executes it.

RStudio also has an autosave feature that saves you R script upon exiting R. This allows you peace of mind, knowing that you can always come back to your work at exactly the same place you left it off. This book does highly recommend the use of comments with the # symbol when writing code in your R script. Comments are a great way to remind you of what a specific line of code was written to achieve.

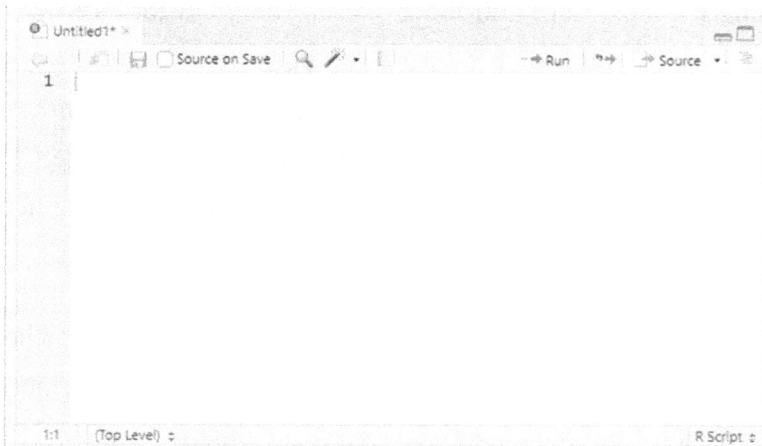

Creating chains with pipes

In addition to using R scripts, you will find the use of pipes to be a good way to make our code easier to know. What are pipes in R? Pipes, as seen by using the symbol %>%, are effectively a way for you to tell R "and then." Officially part of the magrittr package, pipes come loaded in with the Tidyverse. Pipes are incredibly handy due to their ability to link multiple functions into a chain.

Using pipes, let us create a new data frame from the Palmer Penguins raw dataset that gives us the number of males and females of each species of penguin. Notice that with the use of a pipe, you can simplify your code by only having to call upon the Palmer Penguins data set once.

```
> penguins_raw %>% group_by(Species) %>%
count(Sex)
# A tibble: 8 x 3
# Groups:   Species [3]
  Species
      Sex          n
  <chr>
      <chr>   <int>
1 Adelie Penguin (Pygoscelis adeliae)
      FEMALE      73
2 Adelie Penguin (Pygoscelis adeliae)
      MALE        73
3 Adelie Penguin (Pygoscelis adeliae)
      NA          6
4 Chinstrap penguin (Pygoscelis antarctica)
FEMALE      34
5 Chinstrap penguin (Pygoscelis antarctica)
MALE        34
```

```
6 Gentoo penguin (Pygoscelis papua)
    FEMALE      58
7 Gentoo penguin (Pygoscelis papua)
    MALE        61
8 Gentoo penguin (Pygoscelis papua)
    NA           5
```

Summarising data

Now that the previous example utilized two functions not mentioned in this book until this point. Those being the group_by() function and the count() function. Both of these functions, along with the summarise () function, are part of the dplyr package and allow you to summarise a dataset by collapsing variables.

The group_by() function changes the way other functions interact with a dataset by creating groups based on the values of the column you have applied the group_by() function on. When used on its own, you will notice that group_by() doesn't make any noticeable changes to a dataset, but when chained to another function with a pipe, group_by() allows us to make comparisons we otherwise would have to wrestle with to make.

```
# group_by() when used alone
> group_by(penguins_raw, Species)
# A tibble: 344 x 17
# Groups:    Species [3]
    studyName `Sample Number` Species
       Region Island  Stage
    <chr>              <dbl> <chr>
       <chr>  <chr>    <chr>
 1 PAL0708                    1 Adelie
Penguin~ Anvers Torger~ Adult, ~
```

```
 2 PAL0708                    2 Adelie
Penguin~ Anvers Torger~ Adult, ~
 3 PAL0708                    3 Adelie
Penguin~ Anvers Torger~ Adult, ~
 4 PAL0708                    4 Adelie
Penguin~ Anvers Torger~ Adult, ~
 5 PAL0708                    5 Adelie
Penguin~ Anvers Torger~ Adult, ~
 6 PAL0708                    6 Adelie
Penguin~ Anvers Torger~ Adult, ~
 7 PAL0708                    7 Adelie
Penguin~ Anvers Torger~ Adult, ~
 8 PAL0708                    8 Adelie
Penguin~ Anvers Torger~ Adult, ~
 9 PAL0708                    9 Adelie
Penguin~ Anvers Torger~ Adult, ~
10 PAL0708                   1C Adelie
Penguin~ Anvers Torger~ Adult, ~
# ... with 334 more rows, and 11 more
variables:
#    Individual ID <chr>, Clutch Completion
<chr>, Date Egg <date>,
#    Culmen Length (mm) <dbl>, Culmen Depth
(mm) <dbl>,
#    Flipper Length (mm) <dbl>, Body Mass (g)
<dbl>, Sex <chr>,
#    Delta 15 N (o/oo) <dbl>, Delta 13 C
(o/oo) <dbl>,
#    Comments <chr>
```

The count() function in dplyr is a "simple function" that, when related to a column in a data set, prints out a count of each unique value found within that data set. While it gave us a count of the sexes of each penguin species when chained with the group_by()

function, when used alone on the "Sex" column, count() will print a count of all of the sexes together.

```
count(penguins_raw, Sex)
# A tibble: 3 x 2
  Sex        n
  <chr>    <int>
1 FEMALE    165
2 MALE      168
3 NA         11
```

For summarising ()function dplyr allows for both English spellings for the word summarise, so regardless of whether you type out the function as summarising () or summarise(), R will produce the same result. What the summarise () function does, however, is collapse an entire data set's column down to a single row. Like the group_by() function, the summarise () function provides much more value when chained with another function. In the example below, we summarise the Palmer Penguins dataset by averaging the total flipper length of all penguins with the mean() function.

Note the use of the argument "na.rm = TRUE", This argument simply informs R to ignore any values of NA that would otherwise break our summary.

```
 > penguins %>% summarize(
avg_flipper_length = mean(flipper_length_mm,
na.rm = TRUE))
# A tibble: 1 x 1
  avg_flipper_length
                <dbl>
1               201.
```

When chaining the exact same line of code with a group_by() function applied to the species column, you find that R prints out a table of the average flipper length of each species.

```
> penguins %>% group_by(species) %>%
summarize(
avg_flipper_lengtmean(flipper_length_mm,
na.rm = TRUE))
# A tibble: 3 x 2
  species avg_flipper_length
  <fct>              <dbl>
1 Adelie               190.
2 Chinstrap            196.
3 Gentoo               217.
```

Chapter 10

Visualizing Data

Cleaning and manipulating data is incredibly important and useful, but trying to explain your excitement and discoveries to someone without any interest in data analysis or R programming can be quite tough to do based on data frames and tables alone. Like creating a presentation of any kind, using visualizations to quickly and easily understand a

```
> ggplot(data = "Data frame you wish to
visualize") +"geom_function"(mapping = aes(
"various aesthetics including data mappings"
)
dataset's deeper story is vital to analyzing
data properly.
```

While base R has methods of creating visualizations, this book will focus on the use of the ggplot2 package found within the Tidyverse. ggplot2 features an extremely easy-to-understand syntax while also being incredibly versatile in the kinds of visualizations it can create. ggplot2 achieves this with its reliance on what it calls the grammar of graphics.

Much like the rest of the Tidyverse packages, each function found within the ggplot2 package follows a set syntax, making the process of creating your visualizations that much easier. At its core ggplot2 follows this pattern:

Effectively, to create a visualization with the ggplot2 R package, all you would need to do is replace the red text in the pattern above with your required data frame, ggplot function, and then your specific data points (such as the x/y axes). From there, you can execute your code, and R will create your visualization for you. A basic visualization, but a visualization nonetheless. To create more complex visualizations, the ggplot2 package features an incredibly robust array of functions that you will be able to use to customize your visualization further. Be it a bar chart, scatterplot, histogram, or whatever visualization you need. Chances are, the code you will utilize will feature the ggplot2 package.

Preparing your data to be visualized

Let us begin our first data visualization by taking a look at the Palmer Penguins data again. What if we wanted to produce a conception that shows the difference in the average weight of each species of penguin? In order to create this visualization, we need first to check to see if we have the data needed in order to make it. Let us take a glimpse at the Palmer Penguin data set.

```
> glimpse(penguins)
Rows: 344
Columns: 8
$ species        <fct> Adelie, Adelie,
Adelie, Adelie, Adelie, ~
```

```
$ island          <fct> Torgersen, Torgersen,
Torgersen, Torgers~
$ bill_length_mm <dbl> 39.1, 39.5, 40.3, NA,
36.7, 39.3, 38.9, ~
$ bill_depth_mm  <dbl> 18.7, 17.4, 18.0, NA,
19.3, 20.6, 17.8, ~
$ flipper_length_mm <int> 181, 186, 195, NA,
193, 190, 181, 195, 1~
$ body_mass_g    <int> 3750, 3800, 3250, NA,
3450, 3650, 3625, ~
$ sex            <fct> male, female, female,
NA, female, male, ~
$ year           <int> 2007, 2007, 2007,
2007, 2007, 2007, 2007~
```

You will notice quickly that the Palmer Penguins dataset has a column that lists the body mass in grams of each individual penguin observation and a column that lists the species of each penguin as well. You may have already made the connection between this problem and the example of the summarise () function found in the previous chapter. If not, do not worry. These connections will become more clear the more you practice your R programming and data analysis. All you need to do is create a new data frame that groups the Palmer Penguin data by species and then summarises them by average body mass. Like so:

```
> avg_species_weight <- penguins %>%
group_by(species) %>% summarize( avg_weight
= mean(body_mass_g, na.rm = TRUE))
# Let's take a quick look at our new data
frame
> avg_species_weight
# A tibble: 3 x 2
  species    avg_weight
```

```
    <fct>            <dbl>
1 Adelie           3701.
2 Chinstrap        3733.
3 Gentoo           5076.
```

You will notice that in the table printed by R, the values of each average weight are rounded to the nearest whole number. You can use the View() function on the avg_species_weight data frame to see the actual values within the data frame.

Bar Charts in ggplot2

Now that you have prepared your data by creating a data frame that contains the data points needed to answer the question "what is the average weight in grams of each species of penguin" you can easily visualise it with the use of the ggplot2 pattern listed above. With the data frame created and the X and Y aesthetics simply being the avg_species_weight columns, all you need to be left is your geom_function(). In this case, we will use the function geom_col(). The geom_col() function simply just informs R that the visualisation we want to be created is a column-based bar chart.

Note: There is also a geom_function called geom_bar(). The difference between these is that geom_bar() will simply provide a bar chart with counts of each specific variable. In this case, if you used geom_bar() with the species column marked as your x-axis, R will create a bar chart of three bars of equal size as each species name only appears once in the data frame.

Many of the "geom" functions found in the ggplot2 package are named in a similarly intuitive fashion as geom_col() and geom_bar(). If you are using Rstudio, it will even suggest each of the various geom_funcitons as soon as you begin to type "geom_." You will notice that barring a few exceptions, each geom_function typically is written as geom_" kind of visualisation you want." With this knowledge and following the ggplot2 pattern, your geom_col() average penguin weight code should look something like this:

```
> ggplot(data = avg_species_weight) +
geom_col(mapping = aes(x = species, y
= avg_weight))
```

Executing this line of code in your console will produce a graphic like this:

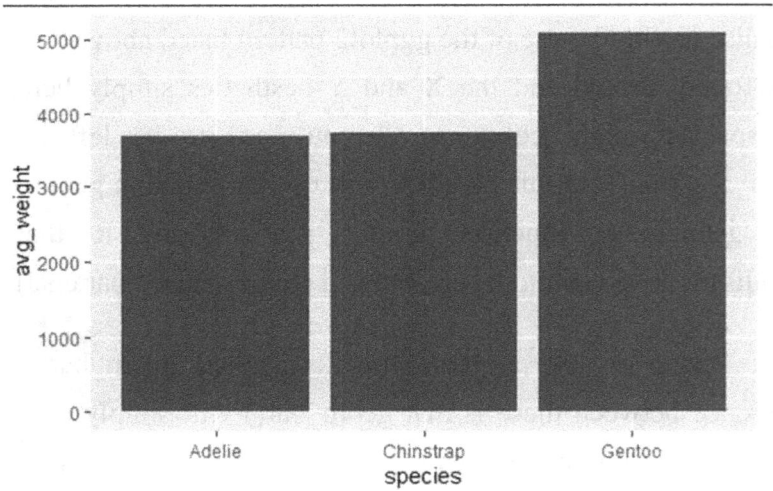

Bar chart without ggplot

A bar chart, often known as a bar graph, is a statistical visual in which numeric data is represented by rectangular bars. The barplot () function in "R" may be used to form a bar chart. To represent

188

frequency according to the required categories, a barplot depicts horizontal or vertical bars parted by white space. Though raw frequencies are often presented, a bar plot may also be used to represent other numbers that are directly dependent on these frequencies, such as means or proportions. The general code for the bar chart is as follow:

Barplot("H", "xlab" , "ylab" , "main" , "names.arg" , "col")

"Ylab" similarly, we will use this to show the labels for the "y-axis"

"Main" is used for the title of" bar chart".

"Names.arg" here, we will show the names for each bar of the chart.

"Col" will be used for colours.

A window with the bar chart will appear when you use this function from the R terminal. You'll need to save your script as an image file if you wish to make a "bar chart." The process is identical to the one described before for creating a pie chart with an R script, except, in Step 2, you must use the barplot() function rather than the pie() function.

Month	Rainfall (mm)
January	28.1
February	27.7

March	95.6
April	63.8
May	18.2
June	11.4
July	49.6
August	39.9
September	13.1
October	63.8
November	11.9
December	73.4

In the above table, I have created some data for monthly rainfall in China. For this example, I just made up some numbers. Now we will plot a bar chart using this data in Rstudio. We already know how we can create a table and assign values to their particular months. Using the following script, I created a bar chart in r studio. Have a look.

```
rain_fall <- c(28.1,27.7,95.6,63.8,18.2,11.4
,49.6,39.9,13.1,63.8,11.9,73.4)
month<- c("jan", "fab",
"mar","apr","may","jun","jul","aug","sep","o
ct","nov","dec")
```

```
barplot(rain_fall, xlab= "year 2022",ylab=
"rainfall(in mm)",
        main = "rainfall data for china",
names.arg = month, col= "green")
```

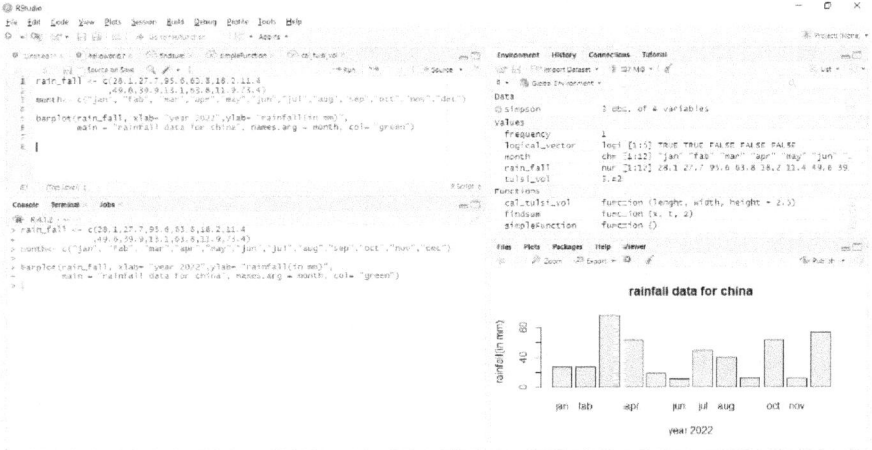

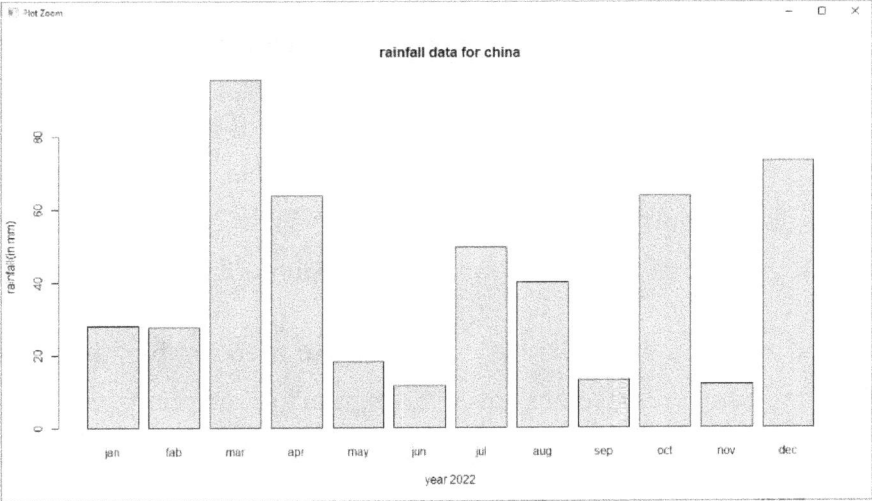

It's not time to develop an R script to generate the bar chart programmatically and export it to an image file now that you know how to draw a bar chart using the R console. We'll save it as "rainfall bar chart.png," color the bars blue, and use only initials for month names.

Histogram

The "barplot" is instinctively comprehensible for calculating numbers in regard to variables in a categorized manner, but it is essentially useless for numeric-continuous variables. A "histogram," an instrument that is commonly mixed up through a "barplot" because it has a related presentation, can be used to show the distribution of continuous measurements. In order to target a numeric-continuous variable, a histogram must first "bin" the observed facts, which means defining "intervals" and then counting the no. of "continuous observations" that occur separately. The bandwidth is the length of this interval.

Consider the rainfall data in China as an example of a "histogram."

For this part, let's say the data of rainfall from that timeframe will be our "population." And consider these numbers to be a sample from that "population." The "hist" program in "R" graphics creates a histogram from a vector of numeric-continuous data.

The sizes of the intervals between them are used to "bin" the data determining the correctness of a "histogram" as a demonstration of the figure of distribution of dimensions. The breaks argument in "hist" controls the bandwidths. You may manually set these by giving each breakpoint a vector and setting it to breaks. The following code accomplishes this by halving the size of each bin from 100 to less than 20 and slightly spreading the total range while using an equally spaced order.

```
rain_fall <- c(28.1,27.7,95.6,63.8,18.2,11.4
,49.6,39.9,13.1,63.8,11.9,73.4)
month<- c("jan", "fab",
"mar","apr","may","jun","jul","aug","sep","o
ct","nov","dec")

hist(rain_fall, xlab= "year 2022",ylab=
"rainfall(in mm)",
        main = "rainfall data for china",
names.arg = month, col= "lightblue")
```

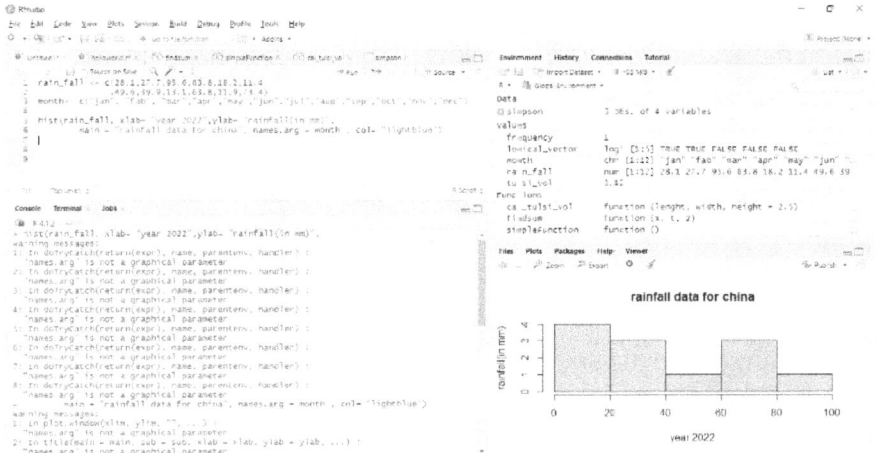

Using the same script, I created this histogram. I just switched *"barplot"* with *"hist."*

The distribution has greater information because of the reduced bandwidth.

Using tighter bins, on the other hand, runs the danger of accentuating "unimportant characteristics." These are most common at points on the scale when data is scant.

You want a width that gives you a decent picture of the scattering of dimensions without accentuating minor details by selecting a "bandwidth" that is too narrow. Similarly, you should avoid obscuring critical elements by employing a "bandwidth" that is too wide.

Pie chart

A "pie chart" is an arithmetical data visualization graphic that divides a circle into slices. Each size's arc length is proportionate to the numerical number it represents. A pie chart may be created in R using the pie() function. For example, we can use the following syntax to create pie charts in R.

pie(numeric value,strings,radius,title,color pallet, clockwise)

Numeric value: in this, you will represent each value of the proportion of the pie slice

Strings: These are the labels that you want to give to each slice of the pie chart.

Radius: these will be the general values that you assign to those strings/labels.

Title: this will be the title of your pie chart—for example, a Demo pie chart or the name of your project.

Colour pallet: in this part, you will assign different colours to the pie chart.

Clockwise: here, you can command the program that how you want your pie chart to be. Either it will be clockwise or anticlockwise.

Only <x> and <labels> are required for all of these parameters; the others are optional. The number of items in <x> should match the number of <labels>.

When invoked from the R terminal, this function opens a window that displays the pie chart. If this function is used from an R script, however, no GUI will be displayed, and the pie chart will be lost. It will have to be saved to an image file programmatically in order to save that pie chart. We'll look at how to accomplish that later in this section; for now, let's look at how to create a pie chart using the R terminal. Consider the following table, which contains fictitious data:

Formation of pie

Labels	Values
Food	142.5
Clothing	46.6
House rent	74.9
Medical	43.5
Others	60

For this example, I am using the above table. Now using the following syntax, I will create a pie chart in R.

```
Label = c( "food" , "clothing" , "medical" ,
"others")
Values = c(142.5 , 46.6 , 74.9, 43.5, 60)
Pie(labels , values, main=( "pie chart" ),
col=("red" , "blue", "green", "orange" ,
"yellow"))
```

Now execute the pie function.

```
Print(pie)
```

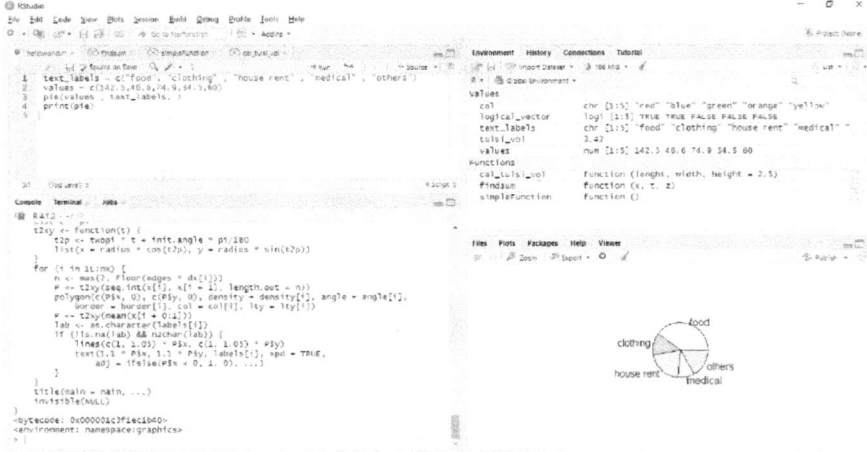

You'll note that when you use the pie function, a new window appears with the pie chart:

So that is how you can create a pie chart using Rstudio. Using the export key, you can save this file and use it in any of your projects.

Let's look at how we may customize the title and color scheme. The *main* parameter may be used to establish the chart's title, and the *col* argument can be used to set the chart's color palette. For example, *main = Pie Chart"* would set the title, and the *rainbow(number>)* function, which outputs a vector of colors, is the ideal approach to define a color palette. As an input, this function requires a number of colors to be utilized. In most circumstances, the number of colors to be utilized will be the same as the number of labels or x vector elements. Alternatively, a vector with color names might be used. For instance, *col = c("red," "blue," "green")*. Using these principles, we'll refer to the pie function as follows, with no modifications to the values or text labels vectors:

```
pie(values , text_labels, main = "pie chart"
, col = c("red" , "blue", "green", "orange"
, "yellow"))
```

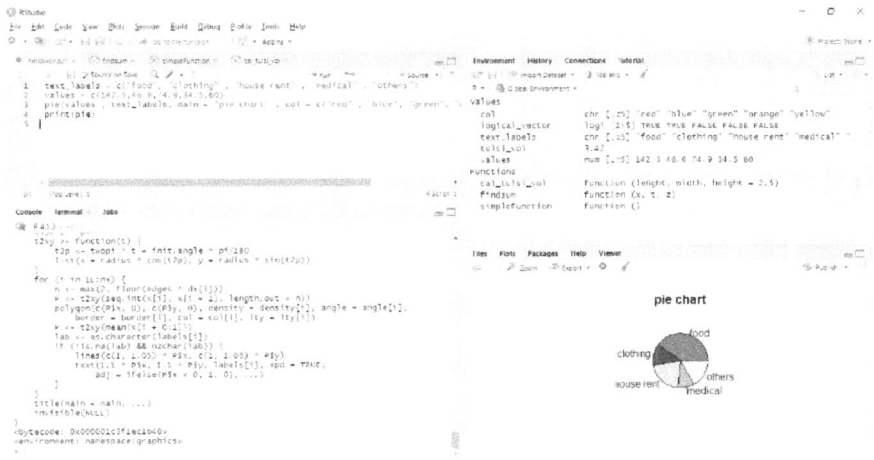

Visualization Aesthetics

You've done it. You have now successfully created your very first data visualization in R to easily share the answer to the Palmer Penguin average weight question. This graphic accurately displays the average weights of each penguin species side by side; however, you have likely thought that you could make a few improvements to this visualization in order to make it much easier to read and quickly understand the information being portrayed by it.

In order to customize and make your visualizations easier to read, ggplot2 features a vast array of commands known as aesthetics. Mapping aesthetics in ggplot2 is your way to add color, shapes, text, and more to your visualization. Now we will make a new chart with the Palmer penguins' data. Maybe you would like to compare the size of each penguin's flipper to their overall body mass? Using the syntax you used to create the last bar chart, try creating a scatterplot with geom_point() and the Palmer penguin data set.

```
> ggplot(data = penguins) +
geom_point(mapping = aes(x =
flipper_length_mm, y = body_mass_g))
```

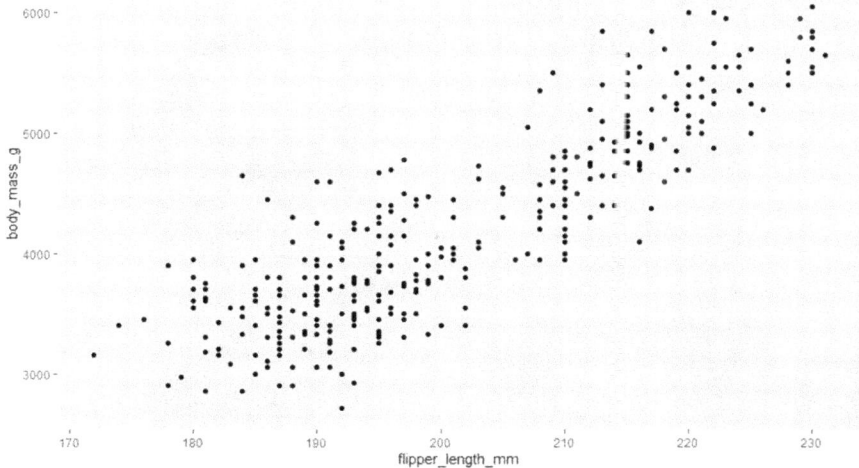

Adding color

This scatterplot alone is very helpful in that you can easily see that there is a trend following the body mass and flipper length of the penguins. Clearly, as a penguin gets heavier, one can safely assume that the penguin's flippers will increase in length accordingly. But what if you would like to differentiate each individual species found in the dataset in this visualization? One way to do that would be to color-code each data point to a related species. You can easily do this with the color aesthetic.

The color aesthetic, like all ggplot2 aesthetics, will be nested within the aesthetic function of ggplot2. You've actually been using the aesthetic function in each of your visualizations thus far by assigning the "X and Y" axes. The aesthetic role of ggplot2 is seen as aes(). Using this knowledge, let us add color to each species in your scatterplot.

```
> ggplot(data = penguins) +
geom_point(mapping = aes(x =
flipper_length_mm, y = body_mass_g, color =
species))
```

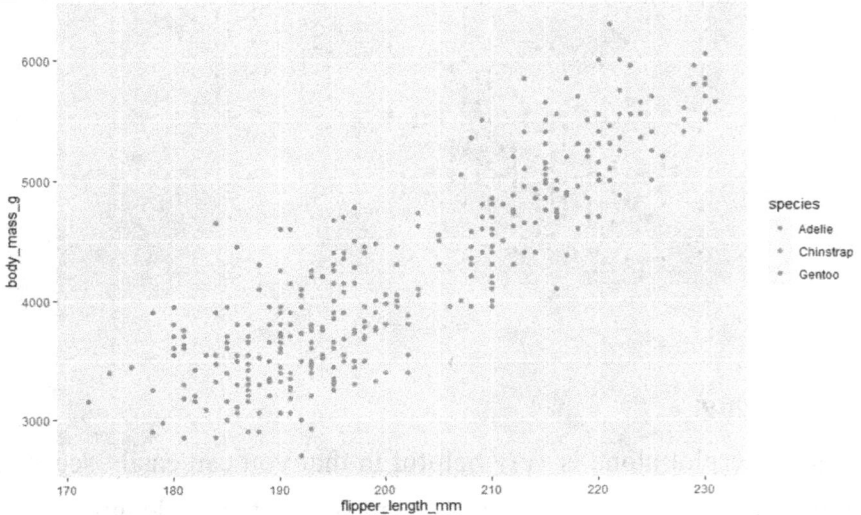

Just like that, R created the same plot as before but with each point automatically assigned a color based on the species column of the Palmer Penguins data set. You will also notice that ggplot2 very smartly also added a new legend to help guide you to understanding what each color means in your new visualization. Using this same pattern, you can use different shapes to differentiate each point like so.

```
> ggplot(data = penguins) +
geom_point(mapping = aes(x =
flipper_length_mm, y = body_mass_g, shape =
species))
```

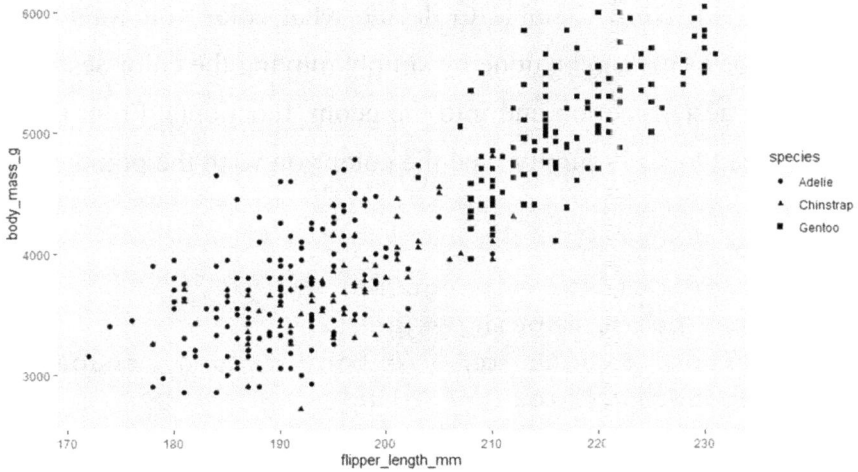

You can also add both shape and color at the same time.

```
> ggplot(data = penguins) +
geom_point(mapping = aes(x =
flipper_length_mm, y = body_mass_g, shape =
species, color = species))
```

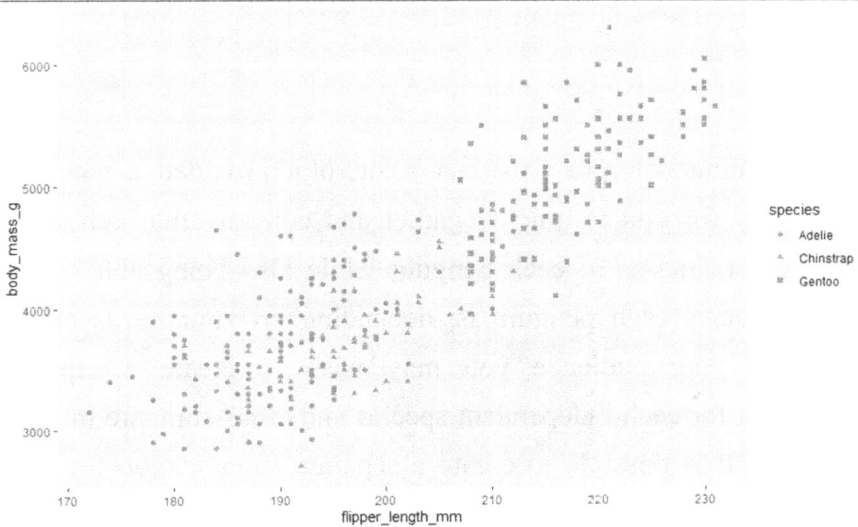

Now, what if you don't like ggplot2's random color choices? What if you would like to be able to decide what color you want your points to be? This can be done by simply moving the color aesthetic out of the aes() function and into the geom_function(). From there, all you need to do is simply type the color you wish the points to be like so:

```
> ggplot(data = penguins) +
geom_point(mapping = aes(x =
flipper_length_mm, y = body_mass_g, shape =
species), color  = "blue")
```

Ggplot2 is great in that is that it doesn't require the use of any complicated color codes. While ggplot2 is more than willing to accept any hexadecimal color codes, one can simply just uses the English word for just about any color they want to add. This is due to ggplot2's clever design, which includes hundreds of easily defined colors, like "Red," "Green," "Orange," and more. Try creating visualizations in tons of different colors using the above syntax.

Facets

While adding color to your last scatterplot provided a nice and quick way for you to quickly gather and compare the body mass and flipper lengths of each penguin while also being able to see which species each penguin is, depending on your needs or the needs of your audience you may wish to create a separate scatterplot for each independent species and cross-compare them in that way. It is possible to create a separate visualization for each and flip through them. Ggplot2 has a faceting feature that makes this much easier for you to do. Simply put, a facet is a small visualization found within a larger visualization concerning a specific subset of data.

ggplot2 features a few different faceting functions that all work very similarly, but for this example, we will be using the facet_wrap() function.

Lets start with our original scatterplot:

```
> ggplot(data = penguins) +
geom_point(mapping = aes(x =
flipper_length_mm, y = body_mass_g, shape =
species, color = species))
```

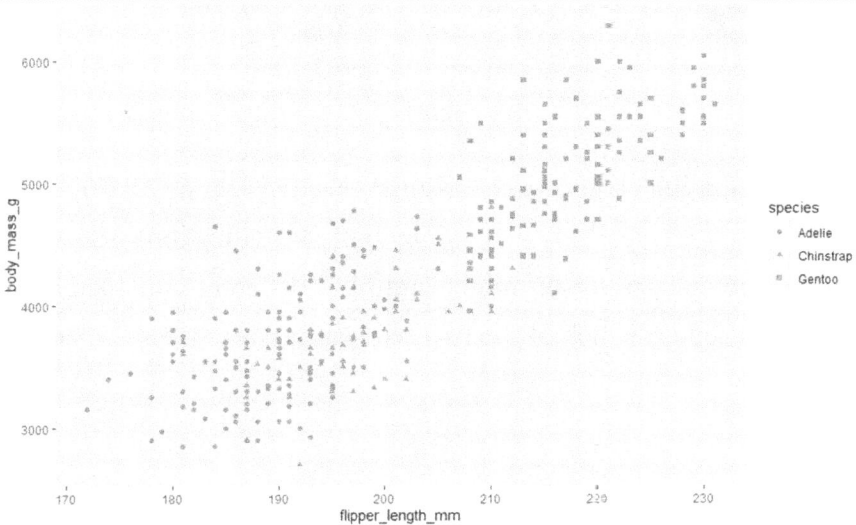

A faceted verison of this same visualization would be written by adding the facet_wrap() function as such:

```
> ggplot(data = puffins) +
geom_point(mapping = aes(x =
flipper_length_mm, y = body_mass_g, shape =
species, color = species)) +
facet_wrap(~species)
```

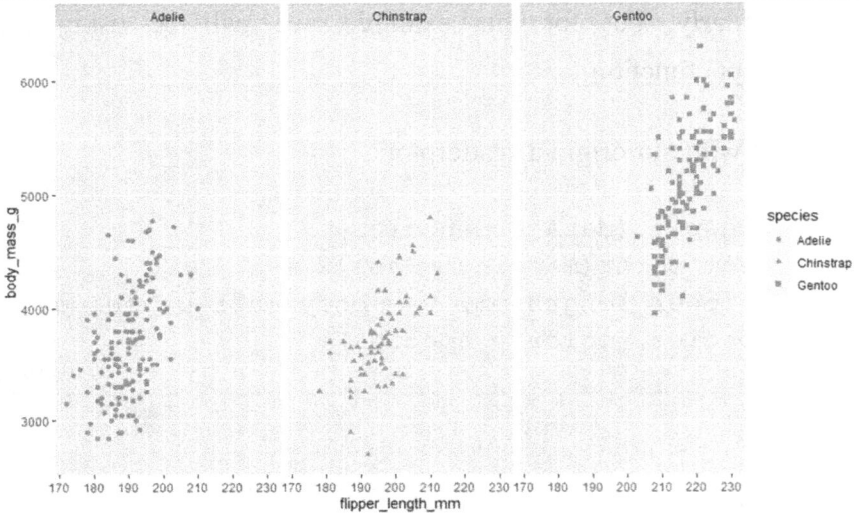

Now comparing both your original scatterplot to the faceted scatterplot, you can see that while both visualizations show the exact same data, a person might highlight different conclusions of the data based on which of the two scatterplots you use.

Conclusion

We've covered the basics of "fundamentals of R programming" in this book, which should be enough to get you started with the language. "R" has a lot of tools for data analysis, data visualization, statistical computation, and other things. If you're in this situation and you want to learn more about any of these topics, please contact us. There are several resources available online. I can assist you in learning more. This is a data-driven era. Huge amounts of data are being collected. Apps, devices, networks, and other sources of data There is a requirement for analyzing this data to help in improved decision-making and decision-making Enhancement of the procedure. I hope you gained something useful from this book. I wish you the best of luck.

Best wishes!

www.ingramcontent.com/pod-product-compliance
Lightning Source LLC
Chambersburg PA
CBHW071601210326
41597CB00019B/3351